RIGHT V. MIGHT

RIGHT V. MIGHT

International Law and the Use of Force

LOUIS HENKIN
STANLEY HOFFMANN
JEANE J. KIRKPATRICK & ALLAN GERSON
WILLIAM D. ROGERS
DAVID J. SCHEFFER

Foreword and Afterword
by
John Temple Swing

COUNCIL ON FOREIGN RELATIONS PRESS

NEW YORK

COUNCIL ON FOREIGN RELATIONS BOOKS

The Council on Foreign Relations, Inc., is a nonprofit and nonpartisan organization devoted to promoting improved understanding of international affairs through the free exchange of ideas. The Council does not take any position on questions of foreign policy and has no affiliation with, and receives no funding from, the United States government.

From time to time, books and monographs written by members of the Council's research staff or visiting fellows, or commissioned by the Council, or written by an independent author with critical review contributed by a Council study or working group are published with the designation "Council on Foreign Relations Book." Any book or monograph bearing that designation is, in the judgment of the Committee on Studies of the Council's board of directors, a responsible treatment of a significant international topic worthy of presentation to the public. All statements of fact and expressions of opinion contained in Council books are, however, the sole responsibility of the author.

Copyright © 1991 by the Council on Foreign Relations®, Inc.
All rights reserved.
Printed in the United States of America.

Library of Congress Cataloguing-in-Publication Data

Right v. Might: international law and the use of force / Louis Henkin
    ... [et al.].–2nd ed.
        p.   cm.
    Includes bibliographical references and index.
    1. Aggression (International law) 2. Intervention (International law) 3. United States—Foreign relations—1945–   I. Henkin, Louis.   II. Title: Right versus might.
JX4471.R54   1991   91-23136
341.6'2-dc20   CIP

92   93   PB   10   9   8   7   6   5   4   3   2

CONTENTS

PREFACE TO THE SECOND EDITION

The second edition of *Right v. Might* includes a new chapter, an afterword, and a revised listing of suggested readings. In Chapter 5, David J. Scheffer examines the U.S. invasion of Panama in 1989, the collective response to the Iraqi invasion of Kuwait in 1990, and the challenges confronting international law and the use of force in what President George Bush has described as the "new world order." In the Afterword, John Temple Swing reflects upon the sea change that has occurred in world politics since the publication of the first edition. He points out that Soviet "new thinking" set the stage for a shift away from U.S. unilateralism so evident in Panama in favor of the collective response that was ultimately mounted against Iraq. He concludes with a brief analysis of the promise but also the pitfalls that lie ahead in the attempt to make collective security a reality in the post–Cold War world.

FOREWORD

John Temple Swing

Man's readiness to settle differences by force of arms has been a feature of society since prehistory. Man's attempt to place rational bounds on the use of force, emerging from his revulsion against the scourge of war, is almost as old. This struggle to impose "rationality on reality" was a central feature of the Enlightenment and the "Age of Reason" in the eighteenth century. It was also central to the debates among the fathers of the American Constitution; one of the fruits of those debates was the separation of powers which, among other things, reserved the power to declare war exclusively to the Congress. The perceived need to "find some better way" was a principal motivation behind American idealism that led to U.S. attempts to introduce arbitration as the preferred method of settling international disputes early in this century, in President Wilson's Fourteen Points, and in American leadership in the creation of the concept of collective security embodied first in the League of Nations and then, at the end of the most disastrous war in history in 1945, in the Charter of the United Nations.

The central contest between reason and force is inescapable today. It arises and will continue to arise in several contexts. One is the continuing dispute between the president and the Congress over the war powers. More importantly, it will lurk in the background of almost every national security decision that President Bush will be called on to make whether in the Middle East, Central America, or in negotiating new arms control agreements with the Soviet Union. Put simply, can we learn to live together under agreed rules, either explicit or tacit, in a world where the tools of destruction—nuclear, chemical, conventional, or terrorist—grow ever more potent and threatening every day? Is it still possible or even desirable to attempt to "substitute reason for force"?

This volume attempts to grapple with these questions. It had its genesis in the invasion of the Caribbean island of Grenada by U.S. troops ordered by President Ronald Reagan in October 1983. Cheered at the time by many as a courageous and incisive act to restore order and keep communism at bay, the invasion was accepted by a majority of Americans as a welcome victory. Following a decade of indecision and ultimate defeat in Vietnam, it arguably did more to reestablish American self-esteem and sense of potency than any single international act since President John F. Kennedy's successful facedown of the Soviets in the Cuban missile crisis two decades earlier.

At the same time, the circumstances surrounding the invasion were deeply troubling to many lawyers whether or not they were trained in international law and whether or not they were supporters or detractors of the president's other domestic and international policies. At issue was the appropriateness of the use of force in a manner that seemed to fly directly in the face of long-standing and legally binding international agreements that constrained the use of force, in the making of which, as already noted, the United States had been the leader following both World War I and II. That commitment is found in a number of international treaties to which the United States remains a party, including the charters of the Organization of American States and the United Nations. The latter, in article 2(4), requires all states "to refrain in their international relations from the threat or use of force against the territorial integrity or political independence of any state. . . . "

Almost immediately following the Grenada invasion, lawyers and commentators on public policy from both sides of the issue found themselves debating the specifics of whether the invasion "lived up" to international law, as well as more general questions such as the proper role of international law in the formulation of American foreign policy. Some even asked whether international law was still relevant in light of the Grenada invasion. Indeed, the entire discipline perhaps reached its nadir in the short-lived public debate over the invasion when *The Wall Street Journal* commented editorially on November 1, 1983, that any international lawyer who questioned the propriety of the invasion should simply "keep his mouth shut"!

With the subsequent withdrawal of U.S. troops from Grenada, what public debate there had been over these issues was eclipsed by other events and tended to die down. Quite appropriately, at the Council on Foreign Relations it did not. For one thing, the Council has had a long tradition of interest in the interaction of law and foreign policy. The organization owes its genesis to the need that U.S. advisors to President Woodrow Wilson perceived at the Versailles Conference for closer American involvement in and understanding of events that had led to World War I and President Wilson's proposal that the League of Nations be formed. In the years since, that tradition has continued in the appointment of Philip Jessup, the eminent international lawyer and U.S. judge on the World Court, as a Whitney Shephardson Fellow in 1970–1971 to write a book on law and politics in U.S. decisions on settlement of international disputes; in the Council's sponsorship of two editions of Professor Louis Henkin's book, *How Nations Behave,* in 1968 and 1979; and in the study project sponsored jointly by the Council and the Association of the Bar of the City of New York that led to the publication in 1985 of *American Hostages In Iran: The Conduct of a Crisis.*

On June 11, 1984, thirty-seven Council members met at the Harold Pratt House to discuss "The Role of International Law in U.S. Foreign Policy: Is It Still Relevant?" Nicholas deB. Katzenbach, former undersecretary of state and deputy attorney general, chaired the discussion, and Professor Richard N. Gardner of Columbia University, Senator Daniel P. Moynihan, and Norman Podhoretz of *Commentary* magazine delivered formal presentations. Participants included lawyers and nonlawyers alike, including editorial writers Robert Bartley of *The Wall Street Journal* and Karl Meyer of *The New York Times;* university professors Arthur Schlesinger, Jr. of CUNY, Joseph Nye of Harvard, and

Richard H. Ullman of Princeton; and syndicated columnist George F. Will.

At the June 1984 meeting a number of questions were raised but not adequately answered. They included basic philosophical issues: what is the nature of international law? Does it even exist? Even if it does, do the ends justify the means? More concrete issues were discussed as well, among them whether norms of collective security were still valid in today's world and under what circumstances "self-defense" or unilateral intervention is permissible.

In an attempt to examine these and other questions, in the fall of 1984 the Council convened a study group on "International Law and the Use of Force" under the chairmanship of William D. Rogers, former undersecretary of state, with lawyer and Council international affairs fellow David J. Scheffer as rapporteur. The group held seven meetings spanning a three-year period from February 1985 to March 1988. A manuscript review session of the group was held in July 1988.

Like the group that had met in June 1984, a majority of study group members attending each session were lawyers, but participants also included scholars, particularly of political science, defense consultants, historians, government officials, and journalists. (The study group members as well as the agenda for each session are listed in the appendix.) The issues which originally had brought these individuals together continued to be illuminated by events subsequent to the Grenada invasion: the shelling of Lebanon by the USS New Jersey, the mining of Nicaraguan harbors by the CIA, covert and overt aid to the contras, the bombing of Libya in 1986, and other acts which continued to generate controversy during the Reagan administration. In particular, following four meetings at which the study group pitted traditional principles of international law against novel theories on the use of force, the members were confronted with the decision of the World Court in *Military and Paramilitary Activities in and against Nicaragua (Nicaragua v. United States of America)*, Merits, 1986 ICJ REP. 14. The World Court's ruling, which introduced a controversial interpretation of international law and conflicted with the central tenets of the Reagan Doctrine, dominated much of the discussion during the final three meetings of the group.

The discussions at every session were lively and provocative and covered so much ground that it would have been impossible to produce a single volume that adequately addressed all the issues raised, much less the varying shades of consensus or lack of it that might have been reached in the process. Yet in the end, we concluded that a useful contribution to the continuing and critically important debate on the interaction of law and policy could be made by publishing the series of essays that follow, each reflecting a different point of view or way of looking at some of the basic issues, and allowing the reader to be the judge.

The Council is deeply indebted to David J. Scheffer, who undertook not only to do the major editing of the volume but contributed an introductory chapter that provides an excellent overview of the issues that the group addressed and sets the scene for the essays that follow by Jeane J. Kirkpatrick and Allan Gerson, Louis Henkin, Stanley Hoffmann, and William D. Rogers. We are also grateful to The Ford Foundation who underwrote the study group and its publication expenses through a generous grant to the Council to foster work generally in the area of international law and organization.

In conclusion, it should be pointed out that, in part due to the rush of events over the past five years, the study group met over a far longer period than is normal for such Council projects. As a result not every member attended every meeting, and even among those who did, some would take sharp issue with some of the analyses and conclusions that follow. Thus it is perhaps more true of this volume than of others published by the Council that the views expressed are those of the authors alone and do not represent study group consensus, of which there is little beyond general agreement on the proposition that "the rule of law" does matter. The differences lie in how that "rule" is defined.

John Temple Swing is currently executive vice president of the Council on Foreign Relations. From 1974 to 1981, he also served as expert consul-

tant on the law of the sea to the Department of State, and as a member of the U.S. delegation to the Third United States Conference on the Law of the Sea. He is the author of numerous articles on public international law and most recently of Impressions of Gorbachev (1988) *and* Afghanistan After the Accords: A Report from Kabul (1988).

INTRODUCTION:
THE GREAT DEBATE OF THE 1980s

David J. Scheffer

During the decade of the 1980s two instruments of state policy—the sword of armed force and the shield of international law—cast long opposing shadows on the battlefield of American foreign policy. While it was morning in America for those who believed in the utility of military intervention to influence international affairs, it was dusk for the architects of the United Nations Charter's prohibition on the use of force. Monuments stand erect reminding us of conflicts in Grenada, Lebanon, Libya, Afghanistan, Cambodia, Angola, and Nicaragua. Each of these conflicts challenged conventional norms and generated another round in the great American debate—namely, how to promote democracy overseas, combat terrorism, and remain faithful to the rule of law.

That debate intensified by mid-1984, following three military interventions in which the United States participated directly. The first was the assault on the Caribbean island of Grenada in October 1983, launched in part to rescue American medical students at a time of near-anarchy, but also resulting in the overthrow of a pro-Soviet regime. The second military intervention occurred in Lebanon, where in late 1983 American firepower was unleashed on targets around Beirut. The U.S. Marine Corps suffered hundreds of fatalities while trying to prop up a fragile government under siege by Muslim militia in a country occupied by the Syrian and Israeli armies.

In the third instance, the Reagan administration orchestrated covert assistance to guerrilla groups fighting to overthrow the Sandinista government of Nicaragua. This included support

1

for the mining of Nicaraguan harbors and for attacks on economic targets inside the country, leading Nicaragua to lodge numerous claims against the United States in the International Court of Justice (World Court).

On April 12, 1984, Jeane J. Kirkpatrick, the U.S. permanent representative to the United Nations, addressed the annual meeting of the American Society of International Law in Washington, D.C. She described a vision that would become the canon of the "Reagan Doctrine":

> Clearly, unilateral compliance with the Charter's rules of nonintervention and nonuse of force are of no consequence to some who have been engaged in pursuing "national liberation" in our times, in Africa and Asia, in the Middle East and in Central America. Certainly this is not what the Charter requires of us. If there is to be a rule of law—and we are as committed to that proposition today as ever in our history and as any other nation in the world—that rule of law must be universally accepted, a day which we would welcome.
>
> But we cannot permit, in defense not only of our country but of the domain of law . . . in which democratic nations must rest . . . , ourselves to feel bound to unilateral compliance with obligations which do in fact exist under the Charter, but are renounced by others. This is not what the rule of law is all about. As we confront the clear and present dangers in the contemporary world, we must recognize that the belief that the U.N. Charter's principles of individual and collective self-defense require less than reciprocity is simply not tenable.[1]

To some, these words were an extraordinary departure from the post–World War II consensus on the international legal rules restraining the use of force. To others, however, Kirkpatrick's views reflected reality and the need to reassess the underlying principles of international law.

The study group on "International Law and the Use of Force" at the Council on Foreign Relations struggled to answer some daunting questions: What are the rules on use of force, and how do we apply them institutionally? To what extent does complying with international law enhance the national security of the United States? Assuming that the United States has an interest in some fairly rigorous set of legal rules on the international use of force, is that interest mainly conservative in character? Or would we be better served by trying to introduce important changes?

Members of the study group (listed in the appendix) voiced a considerable range of opinion. It was apparent that the interpretation of international law had become increasingly factious during the 1980s. The proliferation of different interpretations of international conventions and customary law, clearly reflected in the group's deliberations, meant that the guidance that law traditionally offers policymakers was diminished.

Nonetheless, it is possible to group together certain viewpoints on the relationship between international law and the use of force. These might be described, albeit simplistically, as the traditional, neorealist, allied, and behavioral schools. None necessarily stands in opposition to any other, but among them these viewpoints offer fundamentally different approaches to the future conduct of American foreign policy.

The traditional school preserves the key normative provision of the UN Charter—article 2(4)—as the cornerstone of contemporary international law. Article 2(4) requires all members of the United Nations to "refrain in their international relations from the threat or use of force against the territorial integrity or political independence of any state, or in any other manner inconsistent with the Purposes of the United Nations." The traditionalists view this provision with discriminating deference to what they understand to be the original intent of the framers of the Charter. They find in that original intent the basis for a modern restatement of international law on the use of force.

In 1945 the phrase "use of force" evoked vivid memories of armed attacks, nation against nation, across sovereign borders by the most destructive armies ever assembled on earth. Article 2(4) clearly was meant to prohibit aggressive armed attacks. Article 51 mirrored that intent and established the exception to the rule: "Nothing in the present Charter shall impair the inherent right of individual or collective self-defense if an armed attack occurs against a Member of the United Nations, until the Security

Council has taken measures necessary to maintain international peace and security."

Read together, articles 2(4) and 51 do not outlaw all demonstrable uses of force, particularly for credible reasons of self-defense. For example, the Israeli military raid on Uganda's Entebbe airport on July 3, 1976, had one purpose: to rescue the Israeli passengers of an Air France airliner that had been hijacked over Greece. The Israeli action is often cited as support for the right of a state to take military action to rescue its nationals facing mortal danger within the borders of another state, but to do so solely for humanitarian purposes.

According to most traditionalists, the UN Charter should not be read to forbid the use of every conceivable measure of self-defense against aggressive acts that fall short of classical armed attacks across sovereign borders. Even though Soviet forces never invaded Pakistan during their occupation of Afghanistan, the aggressive character of the Soviet military campaign within Afghanistan, the threat it posed to security in the region, and the occasional Soviet military incursions into Pakistan gave the color of justification for Pakistan (with U.S. support) to provide sanctuary and military assistance to the Afghan resistance fighters.

The traditionalists believe that the rules embodied in articles 2(4) and 51 are flexible enough to respond to evolving technological, military, and political developments and that these existing rules are preferable to anything that the nations of the world could attempt to renegotiate.

Their reasoning rests on both historical and contemporary realities. The rules on use of force are not negotiable law. They flow from the inherent character of the state system. A basic rule is that force will not be used to impose one state's will on another state. If that rule became optional or subject to renegotiation, the existing state structure would be in jeopardy.

The modern nation-state system, which came to maturity in the nineteenth century, favors the international status quo. It tolerates one nation's assistance to another that is threatened by external armed attack or by internal insurgency. But it encompasses no clearly defined right to intervene in support of revolutionary change. Classical international law also recognizes that a conflict may reach a point where the right to aid a government might have to yield to a no-right, where it is no longer clear who the government is in an emerging civil war. The sides may become so balanced that to call one a government and another an insurgency would be patently unresponsive to the facts. The classical rule is that no one may aid either side in a civil war.

A number of traditionalists believe that this rule, with some adjustment, has continuing utility for the United States. In their opinion, good governments worth defending against insurgencies outnumber bad governments worth overthrowing. The United States should not be playing a role in the evolution of a legal concept that inevitably would entitle other governments, particularly from the Soviet bloc, to support insurgencies attempting to overthrow governments that merit American support.

These traditionalists generally believe that where an internal revolution is inimical to U.S. interests but does not directly threaten U.S. security concerns or benefit from external support, there is no unilateral right to intervene with force. In four other scenarios, however, some traditionalists believe that clarifying adjustments to the classical rule may be warranted.

First, the classical rule forbids any unilateral right to use force to overthrow a regime on the sole grounds that it is repressive in character. But traditionalists voice different opinions about whether the use of force is justified to intervene for the purpose of preventing a repressive regime from committing gross violations of human rights, such as genocide or mass political executions, or of rescuing nationals trapped in life-threatening circumstances with the complicity of the repressive regime. In practice, armed intervention to prevent genocide or mass political executions in another nation has been far more difficult to justify (despite the enormity of the crime) than humanitarian intervention to rescue trapped nationals. In theory as well, the classical rule has been bent to accommodate the latter, but not yet the former.

Second, where an outside power has imposed a regime in violation of the fundamental rule against intervention, some traditionalists argue that a third state may have the right to counterintervene to protect the independence and territorial integrity of the "invaded" country, provided that right is exercised in collective self-defense in a manner faithful to the procedural framework of article 51 of the United Nations Charter. This perspective, of course, recognizes the authority of the Security Council as it is described in article 51. The right to counterintervene might especially arise where the initial intervention has deprived the people of the right to decide which government will remain in power. The key to this modification of the classical rule is the convincing character of the intervention that has installed the puppet regime. The more certain and militaristic is the foreign power's intervention, and the more internally irreversible it becomes, the more justifiable may be the right to counterintervene.

A third scenario, skewed to accommodate American concerns, would be the establishment (typically by the Soviet Union or its proxy) in a foreign country of a military base posing a direct threat to U.S. national security. Such a threat, some traditionalists contend, may require the use of force as a legitimate act of preemptive self-defense. But the type of force used is critical under international law. During the Cuban missile crisis of 1962, the Kennedy administration imposed a naval quarantine on Soviet shipping bound for Cuba in part because a plausible legal case could be, and was, made for it. The legal case for an air force strike on the Soviet missile launch facilities in Cuba would have been more difficult to make. Similarly, the arrival of a militarily significant number of Soviet attack aircraft at an air base in Nicaragua might warrant, following the collapse of diplomatic methods, a surgical strike by U.S. military aircraft to cripple the Soviet planes. It would be much harder to legally justify a full-scale military invasion of Nicaragua in response to such a deployment. This adjustment to the classical rule, then, is a qualified one that relies heavily on the principle of proportionality and necessity.

Finally, some traditionalists argue that nuclear blackmail used to coerce a state may legitimately be encompassed by article 2(4) and thus may entitle the threatened state to take preemptive military action. Because no clear example of such blackmail has emerged since the dawn of the nuclear age, this adjustment remains strictly theoretical and, luckily, untested. The Cuban missile crisis might have evolved into a case of nuclear blackmail (by both Moscow and Washington) had it not been defused. The Israeli air strike on an Iraqi nuclear facility in 1981 responded not to blackmail, but to the fear of blackmail or worse. At the time, few traditionalists rose to defend the Israeli action as a justifiable use of force. Another type of blackmail, the threat to use chemical or biological weapons or to launch ballistic missiles with conventional warheads, looms as another possible justification for preemptive military action.

According to some traditionalists, these four scenarios, which would justify using force to protect state sovereignty from real or anticipated external intervention or to permit some types of humanitarian intervention, should be accommodated within the framework of articles 2(4) and 51.

The traditionalists draw the line between themselves and others, notably the neorealists, on two key issues. First, they deny the United States a unilateral right to use force under many of the circumstances favored by the neorealists. They point out, for example, that the neorealists' claim to a right to intervene unilaterally on behalf of democracy or against repression raises a host of subjective determinations. The traditionalists caution against a world in which every government can determine the right of intervention on the basis of its own definitions of "repressive" and "democratic." Any rule of intervention on behalf of democracy either would not be generally accepted or would be accepted only on terms defined by every government in its own way, thereby becoming both meaningless and dangerous.

Second, the traditionalists deny that a principle of reciprocity, espoused by the neorealists, should dictate whether the United States complies with rules on the use of force. The fact that the Soviet Union often fails to adhere to these rules does not necessarily justify abandoning them. If the United States followed the Soviet lead of noncompliance, there no longer would be any realistic need to state obligatory international law. We would enter a Hobbesian world.

This debate between the traditionalists and the neorealists actually was tested in a court of law with the case of *Military and Paramilitary Activities in and against Nicaragua (Nicaragua v. United States of America)*.[2] While some traditionalists believe that the World Court strengthened the classical rules on use of force with its 1986 decision in that case, others contend that the court threw a wrench into the long-running debate over article 2(4) of the UN Charter that now will be difficult to dislodge.

The World Court premised its ruling against the United States on a distinction between "armed attack" and "use of force." It essentially held that under current international law, if a state intervenes in the internal affairs of another state by acts of force that constitute armed attack, there is a right to individual or collective self-defense. The legal rationale the U.S. government used for assisting the guerrillas fighting the Sandinista government (contras)—collective self-defense under article 51—lacked the requisite justification: an armed attack by the Nicaraguan army against El Salvador. The court ruled that if acts of force fall short of an armed attack under article 51, then countermeasures (including forcible countermeasures but not armed counterattack) may be taken only by the victim state (El Salvador). Not only had the United States violated the rule forbidding third states from launching countermeasures, but American military and logistical support for the contras exceeded the limits of "forcible countermeasures" and constituted an illegal armed counterattack.

For over forty years, a struggle has been under way to contain the right of self-defense under article 51 to one against armed attack. The aim has been to prevent armed counterattack under article 51 from becoming an all-purpose antidote to the illegal use of any kind of force. But in an apparent effort to honor this objective, the World Court may have muddied the waters with its decision in *Nicaragua v. United States of America*.

The court, without providing any definitional criteria, introduced the ambiguous concept of "forcible countermeasures," which fall short of armed counterattack. It further banned a third state from participating in forcible countermeasures against an aggressor state.

This poses two dilemmas for proponents of the UN Charter. At what point do "forcible countermeasures" violate the ban on the "use of force" under article 2(4)? May third states respond to aggression against an ally only when a classical armed attack occurs?

We are left, some traditionalists argue, with an erroneous presumption that below a certain threshold there is no right to respond to an armed attack (of whatever character) in kind. They believe that because no clean dividing lines are evident when it comes to the use of force, the time-honored rules of proportionality and necessity are sufficient to legitimize forcible responses to aggressive acts of force. These traditionalists also find it perplexing that the World Court appeared to hold that the principle of collective self-defense does not extend to the application of forcible countermeasures. The danger, as they see it, is that articles 2(4) and 51 could become unfathomable edicts.

Despite these shortcomings in the court's decision, the traditionalists recognize its reaffirmation of legal prohibitions on the use of force at a time when those prohibitions are under siege. The next step, according to some traditionalists, is a further restatement of principles embodied in the UN Charter so that "forcible countermeasures" do not violate article 2(4) and collective self-defense is not limited solely to armed counterattack in response to an armed attack on a victim state.

The neorealists view the current state of international law quite differently. For them, the world has changed. Article 2(4) originally fit into the larger scheme of peacekeeping, decision-making, and enforcement under the Charter. But the Charter mechanisms, especially collective self-defense, have decayed. It is clear, the neorealists argue, that the system did not work. The assumptions guiding the Charter's drafters in 1945 have changed dramatically. Political upheavals have radically altered international organizations. Technological progress has revolutionized international politics. No consensus exists between the superpowers that would make the United Nations really work.

The neorealists do not go so far as to advocate abandoning article 2(4). They believe that America's goal should be to give teeth to the article so that it may achieve the status of a legal norm. The problem at the United Nations is that the U.S. views on international law and the use of force have been radically different from those of the Soviet Union and many other member-states. The belief that by strict compliance with all of the provisions of the Charter, the United States will induce others to follow suit is fallacious, according to the neorealists. The failure of that strategy is, they say, an empirical fact.

What method will give the United States the best opportunity to induce others to comply with article 2(4) as interpreted by the neorealists? They argue that the best method is to make clear to adversaries that the United States will respond in accordance with the principle of reciprocity and that article 51 justifies reciprocity. If the United States fails to confront force with force and match intervention with counterintervention, the neorealists caution, the entire international legal order will be in jeopardy.

The principle of reciprocity advocated by the neorealists legitimizes certain standards of state conduct not necessarily sanctioned by customary or codified legal norms or, in light of *Nicaragua v. United States of America*, by the World Court. First, the neorealists urge unilateral military intervention (direct or indirect) by the United States in response to Soviet bloc intervention in other countries. They rarely suggest that the United States be inhibited in responding with force by the procedural requirements of the UN Charter or other multilateral charters. Peaceful means of settling international disputes, particularly through diplomacy, are balanced equally with the use of force. Although the neorealists invoke article 51 to justify almost any use of force by the United States, collective self-defense is not a prerequisite to U.S. intervention in conflicts that have no plausible direct impact on the nation's security.

Second, the neorealists see the use of force as an effective instrument to further other principles that they believe are integral to the UN Charter: self-determination, human rights, and, above all, democracy. The Reagan Doctrine is an expression of this belief. The neorealists reject any norm of international law that would forbid military assistance (including direct American intervention) to a prodemocratic insurgency fighting to overthrow a totalitarian government dependent upon external support. Their doctrine encourages the United States to determine unilaterally which insurgency merits military support and how that support can be provided and used.

The neorealists' point of view poses an intriguing paradox. On the one hand, they challenge the legitimacy of long-held views about international law, such as the prohibitions on aiding insurgencies fighting established governments and intervening on behalf of either side in a civil war. On the other hand, they want to unleash the United States to enforce international law unilaterally.

In the 1980s, the neorealists significantly influenced American foreign policy. As early as 1985, in his State of the Union address, President Reagan described the doctrine named after him with the pregnant claim, "Support for freedom fighters is self-defense and totally consistent with the OAS Charter."[3] But it was not until October 25, 1988, during a speech at Fort McNair, Washington, D.C., that Reagan acknowledged the popular name attached to that doctrine:

> Around the world, in Afghanistan, Angola, Cambodia and, yes, Central America, the United States stands today with those who would fight for freedom. We stand with ordinary people who have had the courage to take up arms against Communist tyranny. This stand is at the core of what some have called the Reagan Doctrine.[4]

The challenge for the neorealists is to convince the rest of the world that the Reagan Doctrine embodies a rule of international law.

Bridging the traditionalist and neorealist points of view is the allied school. The proponents of this school ask whether the United States can defend its vital interests and the freedom of the Western world within traditional international law princi-

11

ples. If it cannot, should the United States develop new rules of international law that have legitimacy? Or should it simply acknowledge that its vital interests can no longer be defended by a principled approach and that it will frequently have to act outside the law?

The allied school, in short, would create among allied Western nations a new multilateral legal order that would embody Western democratic traditions and legitimize the use of force to protect that order. Proponents stress that a nation's power is derived not only from its armaments, but also from its reputation, the kind of legitimacy it can find in support of the things it does, the strength of its alliances, and the degree to which it is viewed in a different light from that of its principal adversaries.

The starting point for the allied school is the UN Charter, whose full meaning is not immediately self-evident from the text alone. Like the U.S. Constitution, the Charter is an ever-expanding document that must respond to a rapidly changing world, one where the collective security arrangement of the immediate post–World War II era has collapsed. In the view of the allied school, the general words of the Charter must be pragmatically read in light of changing circumstances in a turbulent world. That means revising international law so that it remains compatible with the foreign policy objectives of the United States and its allies.

Such an undertaking probably would entail a broader, more flexible standard for the use of force in defense of Western interests. It might also prohibit, for example, any interpretation of international law that would make it impossible for the State of Israel to exist or defend itself. Whether the end product would be international law any longer is open to serious question. But the allied school believes in the rule of law and in the legitimacy of the Western democratic tradition. Combining the two into a supranational law shared by like-minded peoples appeals to those who support both the UN Charter and the use of force for democratic ideals.

Finally, many experts, particularly outside of the legal profession, look to the actual behavior of the superpowers for de facto rules on the use of force. The argument that because you have rules you therefore have law is, in their opinion, a non sequitur. "Rules of behavior" in fact exist among states, particularly between the United States and the Soviet Union. These rules evolve outside of formal lawmaking processes, but often are more important in guiding the conduct of nations.

Rules of behavior include such norms of competition as reciprocal expansions of political influence by the superpowers, bilateral agreements effectively declaring certain countries off-limits to superpower competition, agreement on operational rules of engagement so as to avoid certain forms of intervention, and tacit and verbalized norms that fall short of contractual arrangements but promote patterns of understanding and restraint.

In particular, the Soviet Union and the United States have developed certain patterns of restraint that are remarkable compared with relations between great powers in previous periods of history. Of course, this may be the natural consequence of the post–World War II nuclear standoff between the two superpowers. Whatever the reason, neither has initiated the use of force against the other's territory or military assets. As a corollary, both superpowers have avoided direct confrontation where possible, and neither has put the other in a position where the only choice is between shooting and acceptance of a major humiliation. Even in response to Stalin's blockade of Berlin in 1948, the Berlin airlift, the Cuban missile crisis of 1962, and perhaps Afghanistan in 1988, each side left the other escape hatches. Overall the rules of behavior that have evolved between the United States and the Soviet Union have minimized the use of force by either superpower against the interests of the other.

The distinguished contributors to this book examine the merits of these viewpoints and offer some guidance for the future development of international law and its relevance to the use of force. In chapter 1, Jeane J. Kirkpatrick and Allan Gerson provide an authoritative explanation of the Reagan Doctrine and its intended impact on international law. They approach their task from unique vantage points. Kirkpatrick, a professor of government at Georgetown University, was the U.S. permanent representative to the United Nations from 1981 to 1985 and was instrumental in developing the policy and legal rationales for the Reagan Doctrine. Gerson, an international legal expert now associated with the American Enterprise Institute, was counsel to the U.S. mission to the United Nations and also participated in the development of the Reagan Doctrine. Kirkpatrick and Gerson view the Reagan Doctrine as a reaffirmation of a traditional American doctrine, reflected in the UN Charter, that legitimate government is based on respect for individual rights and the consent of the governed. In their opinion, American leaders' belief that all people deserve such government did not die with the signing of the Charter in 1945. The Reagan Doctrine is consistent, Kirkpatrick and Gerson argue, with the Charter's commitments to the furtherance of democratic self-determination and human rights. Their chapter provides insight into the intellectual basis of a doctrine that no doubt will continue to have an impact on U.S. foreign policy during the Bush administration.

In chapter 2, Louis Henkin of Columbia University's School of Law offers a concise survey of international law as it relates to the use of force. He is a leading authority on international law and the author of several major works in the field, including the Council on Foreign Relations Book *How Nations Behave* (2nd ed., 1979). Henkin examines the law on use of force embodied in the UN Charter, efforts to reconstrue the Charter, various recommended exceptions to the prohibitions of article 2(4), the World Court's ruling in *Nicaragua v. United States of America,* the problems of state compliance, and the legal challenges the Reagan Doctrine poses for American foreign policy. He concludes that the law of the Charter is here to stay, that the Reagan Doctrine should be abandoned, and that, if it again proves necessary, the United States should recommit itself to the Truman Doctrine— namely, the right "to help secure democracy by assistance to an incumbent democratic government against armed attack, direct or indirect, or even against internal rebellion."

Stanley Hoffmann of Harvard University, author of several books on international law and politics, focuses in chapter 3 on the rules of behavior established and observed by the superpowers. He points out that the law of the UN Charter and the various international conventions that deal with the use of force embody moral codes. But informal arrangements that regulate the balance of power between the United States and the Soviet Union also reflect moral concerns. Hoffmann distinguishes between "existential" and "deliberative" rules, the former being the rules of nuclear deterrence and of competition and the latter being the operative rules to carry out the existential ones. He examines the ethical implications of these rules, weighing their positive against their negative aspects. Hoffmann concludes by finding little political or ethical justification for the Reagan Doctrine. He believes that the United States will have to play a major role in the establishment of ethically legitimate rules of the game while the Soviet Union undergoes extraordinary changes internally and in its external behavior.

In the concluding chapter, the study group's chairman, William D. Rogers, examines many of the hard realities confronted by international law since World War II and the achievements of both formal and informal lawmaking in the global arena. Rogers is an international lawyer who served as assistant secretary of state for inter-American affairs and undersecretary of state for international economic affairs in the Ford administration. He points out that war has been a common feature of the postwar landscape, but that a supreme achievement of the community of nations has been the avoidance of World War III. Constraints on and opportunities for the use of force, by superpowers and by small states, have been dramatically altered since Hiroshima. In some important respects, the growing disproportion between the destructive power nations could deploy and the force they actually use is reflected in the vibrancy of legal principles. Rogers notes that the imprecision of the UN Charter's principles breeds evasion. He admits that article 2(4) has become the abstract standard against which uses of force have been and can be notionally measured. But he contends that it, along with article 51, is only one point on the spectrum of undertakings, formal and informal, that restrain the use of force in international affairs. Rogers cautions against a preoccupation with the question of whether all effective restraints are law per se. Rather, he emphasizes the contribution that modest, but precise, instruments of agreement and concord can have in reining in the dogs of war.

As the decade of the 1980s closes, the landscape of American foreign policy is dominated by the presence of Soviet President Mikhail Gorbachev, particularly with respect to the relationship between international law and the use of force. In Gorbachev's address before the United Nations General Assembly on December 7, 1988, which Rogers also notes, the Soviet leader brought to the forefront of his country's foreign policy and world public attention a utopian but nonetheless provocative proposal. "It is obvious," he said, "that the use or threat of force no longer can be or must be an instrument of foreign policy. This applies above all to nuclear arms but that is not the only thing that matters. All of us, and primarily the stronger of us, must exercise self-restraint and totally rule out any outward-oriented use of force." Later in his speech, Gorbachev proposed "a world community of States which are based on the rule of law and which subordinate their foreign policy activities to law."[5]

These were not novel ideas. For several years Soviet diplomats and Soviet legal scholars have addressed these issues of law and military force from an increasingly enlightened point of view. Given the history of Soviet conduct in world affairs, however, American and allied skepticism has been entirely valid.

But Gorbachev's stated commitment to the rule of law, coupled with evidence of internal restructuring and varied degrees of Soviet withdrawal from areas of regional and strategic conflict, may add a hopeful new dimension to the debate over international law and the use of force. Whatever course American foreign policy takes in the 1990s, the lessons of the preceding decades, which this book attempts to address, will be at the center of that debate.

NOTES

1. Address by Jeane J. Kirkpatrick, *Proceedings of the Seventy-Eighth Annual Meeting of The American Society of International Law,* Washington, D.C., April 12–14, 1984 (The American Society of International Law, 1986), pp. 67–68.
2. Judgment on the Merits, 1986 ICJ REP. 14; also published in *International Legal Materials,* vol. 25 (September 1986), pp. 1023–1289.
3. "Address Before a Joint Session of the Congress on the State of the Union, February 6, 1985," *Public Papers of the Presidents of the United States: Ronald Reagan, 1985,* Book I (Washington, D.C.: U.S. Government Printing Office, 1988), p. 135.
4. Remarks to the Students, Faculty, and Guests of the National Defense University, and the Signing of the Department of Veterans Affairs Act, October 25, 1988, *Weekly Compilation of Presidential Documents,* vol. 24, no. 43 (October 31, 1988), p. 1368.
5. Statement by Mikhail S. Gorbachev at Plenary Meeting of the United Nations General Assembly, December 7, 1988, provided by the Embassy of the USSR, Washington, D.C. A full text of the statement also is reprinted in *Foreign Broadcast Information Service—Soviet Union,* vol. 88, no. 236 (December 8, 1988), pp. 11–19.

1

THE REAGAN DOCTRINE, HUMAN RIGHTS, AND INTERNATIONAL LAW

Jeane J. Kirkpatrick & Allan Gerson

The doctrine of non-intervention, to be a legitimate principle of morality, must be accepted by all governments. The despots must consent to be bound by it as well as the free States. Unless they do, the profession of it by free countries comes but to this miserable issue, that the wrong side may help the wrong, but the right must not help the right. Intervention to enforce non-intervention is always rightful, always moral, if not always prudent.[1]

John Stuart Mill

A great deal of confusion and disagreement surrounds the idea of the Reagan Doctrine. The term is used to describe the most diverse phenomena. It has been described as covering—and presumably justifying—all cases in which the United States used force during the Reagan administration, including the following:

- the intervention in Grenada in 1983;
- the interception of an Egyptian airliner carrying a suspected attacker of the *Achille Lauro* in 1985;
- the bombing of Libya in 1986;
- the mining of Nicaraguan harbors in 1984.

These events occurred in very different contexts, and the administration offered very different justifications for each of them. Not one of these cases constitutes an example of the application of the Reagan Doctrine. Rather, they are instances in which the administration found it appropriate to use force directly.

19

The United States never justified its action in Grenada in terms relevant to the Reagan Doctrine. That action resulted, the administration explained, from a unique conjunction of events:

- the existence of the Treaty Establishing the Organization of Eastern Caribbean States, which includes a provision for calling on other states for help, and that organization's request to the United States;
- the appeal of the governor-general of Grenada for assistance (which he confirmed);
- the implicit threat to hundreds of American students in a situation of anarchy and violence (which also was repeatedly confirmed).

The Reagan Doctrine also was not relevant to the interception in 1985 of an Egyptian airliner carrying a presumed terrorist responsible for the murder of Leon Klinghoffer on the cruise liner *Achille Lauro*. That action involved apprehending a person believed (with good reason) to be guilty of violent crimes against Americans. The purpose was to bring him to trial by the only means possible.

Neither was the bombing of Libya on April 14, 1986, an expression of the Reagan Doctrine. The administration justified it as an act of self-defense against a campaign of terrorism directed at Americans. Even the mining of harbors in Nicaragua was not a typical application of the Reagan Doctrine, since it involved the direct use of U.S. force.

The Reagan Doctrine, as we understand it, is above all concerned with the moral legitimacy of U.S. support—including military support—for insurgencies under certain circumstances: where there are indigenous opponents to a government that is maintained by force, rather than popular consent; where such a government depends on arms supplied by the Soviet Union, the Soviet bloc, or other foreign sources; and where the people are denied a choice regarding their affiliations and future. The Reagan Doctrine supports the traditional American doctrine that armed revolt is justified as a last resort where rights of citizens are systematically violated. This view is, of course, stated clearly in the Declaration of Independence, which insists that *legitimate* government depends on the consent of the governed.

The Reagan Doctrine opposes traditional isolationism and post-Vietnam assumptions about the illegitimacy of U.S. intervention. It rejects the idea that American power is dangerous to the world. It denies that any use of American power constitutes a first step down a slippery slope to war. It denies the Brezhnev Doctrine's claim that communism is irreversible. It rejects the notion that any government must be respected; that is, it rejects the inviolability of sovereignty.

It is more modest and less sweeping than the Truman and Kennedy doctrines. It is modest because it is effectively limited to those people and places where governments are maintained by externally supplied force and where, in response, insurgencies have arisen. It does not speak to the time, place, or amount of U.S. assistance. All these issues are to be decided by prudential considerations. Most important, the Reagan Doctrine addresses questions of legitimacy.

The debate about the Reagan Doctrine is part of a debate about who we are, about our own identity. It neither advocates nor permits casual use of force. It circumscribes the situations in which the United States may intervene with its assistance in the affairs of others: that is, when no political processes are available to open a system and when repressors use external assistance to keep the system closed.

The Reagan Doctrine expresses *solidarity* with the struggle for self-government as against one-party dictatorship and incorporation by force into the Soviet "socialist world system" or any other international relationship. It does not *require* offering armed resistance. The Reagan Doctrine *permits* it. It does not address the question of U.S. military involvement or involvement of U.S. forces in any particular contest. It is a permissive doctrine that postulates the moral legitimacy of American military aid under certain circumstances. It provides moral guidelines. Policy under the Reagan Doctrine is established by prudential determination of the national interest in particular contexts.

Ronald Reagan articulated what came to be known as the Reagan Doctrine in his 1985 State of the Union address and in his speech at Bitburg Air Force Base on May 5, 1985. At Bitburg he said:

> Twenty-two years ago President John F. Kennedy went to the Berlin Wall and proclaimed that he, too, was a Berliner. Well, today freedom-loving people around the world must say: I am a Berliner, I am a Jew in a world still threatened by anti-Semitism. I am an Afghan, and I am a prisoner of the Gulag. I am a refugee in a crowded boat foundering off the coast of Vietnam. I am a Laotian, a Cambodian, a Cuban, and a Miskito Indian in Nicaragua. I, too, am a potential victim of totalitarianism.[2]

That paragraph is a very clear-cut statement of American *solidarity* with victims of totalitarianism.

In the 1985 State of the Union address, Reagan went beyond asserting solidarity to state the legitimacy of support for the struggle of others, for their independence, and for their self-government. He added the proposition that it is in U.S. interests to offer such support:

> [W]e must not break faith with those who are risking their lives—on every continent, from Afghanistan to Nicaragua—to defy Soviet-supported aggression and secure rights which have been ours from birth. . . . Support for freedom fighters is self-defense . . .[3]

Obviously, the Reagan Doctrine rejects the Brezhnev Doctrine, which asserts the irreversibility of the establishment of Marxist-Leninist governments anywhere. It denies that to assist in overthrowing an existing government is always wrong. The legitimacy of such acts depends on the political and moral context: the nature of the government, the role of foreign force, and the existence of resistance.

The Reagan Doctrine rests on the traditional American doctrine, stated in the Declaration of Independence, that the legitimacy of a government depends on its respect for individual rights and on the consent of the governed. The Declaration's words define that doctrine: "We hold these truths to be self-evident, that all men are created equal, that they are endowed by their Creator with certain unalienable rights, that among these are life, liberty and the pursuit of happiness. That to secure these rights, governments are instituted among men, deriving their just powers from the consent of the governed."

Mirroring basic American constitutional principles, the Reagan Doctrine rests on the claim that *legitimate* government depends on the consent of the governed and on its respect for the rights of citizens. A government is not legitimate merely because it exists, nor merely because it has independent rulers. Nazi Germany had a de facto government headed by Germans; that did not make it legitimate. Nicaragua today has a de facto government headed by Nicaraguans who were not elected in any competitive sense, who came to power by armed force, with help, on the basis of their promise to establish a democracy. It is a government that requires massive foreign military support to maintain its power and to stop the advance of an indigenous armed resistance.

Like most American "doctrines," the Reagan Doctrine emerged in response to circumstances: it was developed in response to the Soviets' objective of a global empire and in response to Soviet claims of legitimacy in their imperial venture embodied in the Brezhnev Doctrine and the doctrine of "national liberation wars." More specifically, the Reagan Doctrine was a response to the Soviet Union's efforts to hurriedly establish Marxist-Leninist governments in Third World countries and incorporate these into its "socialist world system."

The Reagan Doctrine did not seek to roll back existing communist regimes. In the five years preceding Reagan's inauguration, nine *new* Leninist dictatorship states were established around the globe: in South Vietnam, Cambodia, and Laos in 1975; through Mozambique and Angola's forcible conversion to communism later that year; in Ethiopia in 1977; and as the result of a coup d'état in Grenada, civil war in Nicaragua, and the Soviet invasion of Afghanistan following an earlier coup d'état in 1979. In each case, the Soviet Union and the Soviet bloc provided weapons and advice to the emerging Leninist government. Each sought to rule by force and with reinforcements from the Soviet bloc. In each, resistance movements developed: more than 350,000 resistance fighters took up arms in six of the nine Soviet client-states established in the late 1970s.

The Reagan administration did not create these resistance movements. It did not initiate the policy of providing support. The Kennedy and Johnson administrations had provided help in Vietnam and Cambodia, the Nixon administration in Southeast Asia and Angola, and the Carter administration in Afghanistan. But the Reagan administration articulated, in the wake of the Vietnam War, the moral and legal right to provide aid to indigenous resistance movements in countries around the globe, and justified it in terms of traditional American conceptions of legitimacy. This right is related to both "containment" and "roll-back," but is not identical with either.

The Reagan Doctrine addresses such questions as: Is it morally and legally acceptable for the United States to support indigenous armed movements against such governments? Or does such support constitute unjustified and illegal interference in their internal affairs? Does intervention (by the Soviet bloc) justify counterintervention? If so, when?

These general questions lie just beneath the surface whenever Congress considers whether to provide assistance to the contras in Nicaragua, the Mujaheddin in Afghanistan, the Khmer People's National Liberation Front, União Nacional para a Independência Total de Angola, and Resistência Nacional Moçambicana in southern Africa. Obviously, the issues involved here touch directly on some important questions of politics, morals, and international law. Answers to these questions are present in the American conception of legitimacy, and in Wilsonian and Rooseveltian views about the application of these conceptions. The Reagan Doctrine reflects traditional American conceptions. The hostile reaction to it reminds us of the incompatibility of traditional conceptions concerning the use of power with post-Vietnam revisionist views. Some would say that the chief charges against the Reagan Doctrine have been that it violates the UN Charter's prohibitions on interference in the internal affairs of states, its prohibitions against the use of force, and its commitment to the sovereign equality of states.

We believe these charges to be mistaken. However, there is tension between the American view that legitimate government is based on consent and the UN Charter's prohibiting interference in the internal affairs of states. It is true, also, that the United States and the USSR have always had substantially different interpretations of self-determination, sovereign equality, and the circumstances under which it is and is not permissible to use force and to intervene in the affairs of other states.

THE REAGAN DOCTRINE:
A VIOLATION OF THE UN CHARTER?

It has been argued that the traditional American doctrine of legitimacy applies only to the rights of citizens to take up arms against their own government, not to the rights of others to supply arms. Others, it has been argued, are bound by the prohibitions contained in article 2(4) of the UN Charter.

Article 2(4) enjoins all member-states to "refrain in their international relations from the threat or use of force against the territorial integrity or political independence of any state, or in any other manner inconsistent with the purposes of the United Nations." But in the U.S. view it is clear that this prohibition was intended not to stand on its own, but to be seen in the context of the entire Charter, as complementary to article 51 (which affirms the inherent right to individual or collective self-defense) and to all of the provisions concerning guarantees of human rights.

Moreover, the Charter clearly declares that United Nations member-states will respect human rights (which encompass democratic freedoms), be peace-loving, and be committed to the maintenance of world peace. Its whole purpose, as the United States saw it at the time it was promulgated, was to promote a world of just such states and behavior. The UN Charter, which was essentially American in design, was neither created nor viewed as providing a protective shield for the expansion of repressive dictatorships or empires. When the Soviet Union was persuaded to accept the Charter, it was expected eventually to be persuaded to live by these rules.[4]

PREVIOUS PRESIDENTS' UNDERSTANDING OF THE UN CHARTER

President Harry Truman read the UN Charter's permissions and prohibitions in the terms we have described. "I believe," he said in his message of March 12, 1947, to a joint session of Congress, "that it must be the policy of the United States to support free peoples who are resisting attempted subjugation by armed minorities or by outside pressures."[5] These words—which came to be known as the Truman Doctrine—were used to support his request for aid to Greece and Turkey, which were then on the verge of collapse and a takeover by communist guerrillas. Truman chose not to speak of a direct threat to the security interests of the United States or in the language of the UN Charter's reference to armed attack. Instead, he put the issue in terms of the values of the Charter and of the Declaration of Independence.

President John Kennedy, in an October 1962 proclamation, reaffirmed the Truman Doctrine and applied it specifically to the Western Hemisphere, declaring, "[T]he United States is determined to prevent by whatever means may be necessary, including the use of arms, the Marxist-Leninist regime in Cuba from extending, by force or the threat of force, its aggressive or subversive activities to any part of this hemisphere, and to prevent in Cuba the creation or use of an externally supported military capability endangering the security of the United States . . . "[6]

The Truman Doctrine was, as noted earlier, a commitment born of the values enshrined in the Declaration of Independence. And, as President Franklin Roosevelt and Prime Minister Winston Churchill made clear in signing the Atlantic Charter in August 1941, those values of individual liberty were to guide the postwar order they hoped would emerge. Thus the Atlantic Charter expressed the hope for "a peace which will afford to all nations the means of dwelling in safety within their own boundaries, and which will afford assurance that all men live out their lives in freedom from fear and want." The United States championed the new order of the United Nations and never interpreted it as prohibiting a concern about the relations between a government and its citizens. To the contrary, it interpreted the UN Charter's emphasis on human rights as encouraging just such a course.

The American commitment to promotion of democracy as the guide to foreign policy can also be seen in the language of the Inter-American Treaty of Reciprocal Assistance, signed at Rio de Janeiro in 1947 (and hence known as the Rio treaty), and in the Charter of the Organization of American States (OAS), signed at Bogotá in 1948. Both documents were drafted during the period immediately following the drafting of the UN Charter, and in many ways they mirrored that Charter. Their commitment to democracy and the assumption that democracy was a necessary condition of peace, however, was more explicit. Article 5(d) of the OAS Charter "reaffirmed" the principle that "the solidarity of the American states and the high aims which are sought through it *require* the political organization of those States on the basis of the effective exercise of representative democracy" (emphasis added). President Lyndon Johnson's intervention in the Dominican Republic in 1965, after the democratically elected government of Juan Bosch had been overthrown in a military coup, was based on the democratic principles in the Rio treaty and OAS Charter. Johnson defined the U.S. goal in the Dominican Republic as being to permit people of that country "to freely choose the path of political democracy, social justice and economic progress."[7]

The commitment to democracy also guided U.S. actions in the Far East in the post–World War II period. President Dwight Eisenhower refused to sign the 1954 Geneva accords, which partitioned Vietnam, out of fear that it "would probably lead to Communist enslavement of millions."[8] At the final session of the Geneva conference the United States reiterated its "traditional position that peoples are entitled to determine their own future."[9] In 1968, Secretary of Defense Clark Clifford restated the Truman Doctrine's declaration of support for free peoples resisting attempted subjugation by armed minorities or by outside pressure and applied it to Vietnam. He said:

> We are assisting the brave and beleaguered country to fight aggression, under the SEATO Treaty—and for the same reason that we extended our aid to Greece and Turkey over 20 years ago. This is in the tradition of the Truman Doctrine, which announced 20 years ago that we would help defend the liberty of peoples who wished to defend themselves. . . . The America that brought NATO into being is the same America supporting freedom in Asia today—and for the Asians, not for the Americans.[10]

So much for the idea that U.S. support for the struggle for democracy abroad ended with the adoption of the UN Charter. President Reagan's 1985 State of the Union message that "we must not break faith with those who are risking their lives on every continent, from Afghanistan to Nicaragua, to defy Soviet supported aggression and secure rights which have been ours from birth" reiterated a theme sounded in American foreign policy for the last four decades.

The fact that the Truman and Kennedy doctrines were abandoned by certain of their successors does not prove that Truman and Kennedy's understanding of the Charter was mistaken. To the contrary, the issues they confronted became more urgent with the development and expansion of the Soviet empire under Khrushchev and his successors.

THE REAGAN DOCTRINE
AND SELF-DETERMINATION

Obviously, the United States and the Soviet Union interpret the concept of self-determination in different ways. Paraphrasing Lenin, Stalin made clear that "the principle of self-determination must be an instrument in the struggle for socialism and must be subordinated to the principles of socialism."[11] That view—which entailed that the advancement of worldwide socialism would not yield to the UN Charter's proscription of the use of force—has continued to dominate Soviet foreign policy.

This means that by accepting the UN Charter, with its prohibitions on the use of force, the Soviet Union did not abandon its position in support of world revolution. Rather, it chose to pursue a dual foreign policy. To protect security for the USSR and its client-states in a hostile world, Moscow championed the concept of "sovereign equality," according to which all regimes are legitimate and entitled to the same rights. At the same time, the Soviet Union claimed control over Eastern Europe and worked in the UN to redefine existing conceptions of self-determination.

To this end, the Soviet Union transformed the principle of self-determination of peoples in article 1 of the UN Charter from one consonant with the language of the Charter's preamble, which reaffirms "faith in fundamental human rights, in the dignity and worth of the human person," to one that furthers the principle of socialist self-determination. Hence the Brezhnev Doctrine, set out in an article in *Pravda* shortly after the USSR invaded Czechoslovakia in 1968, provided the following:

> There is no doubt that the peoples of the socialist countries and the Communist parties have and must have freedom to determine their country's path of development. However any decision of theirs must damage neither socialism in their country, nor the fundamental interests of other socialist countries, nor the world-wide workers' movement, which is waging a struggle for socialism.[12]

The Soviet army's repression of revolt in Czechoslovakia, as well as its forceful repression twelve years earlier of Hungary's reform efforts, made clear that the Soviet Union would impose distinct limits to self-determination in nations considered within its camp. The Brezhnev Doctrine claimed that the Soviet Union had a right to do so. In the case of Hungary, Soviet armies demonstrated that defection from the bloc was not possible; in the case of Czechoslovakia, they showed that within the bloc incipient democratization that departed from the principle of one-party rule was unacceptable. *Perestroika* notwithstanding, there remain no grounds to believe that the Soviet Union would permit any of the socialist "republics" to reject one-party rule or disengage from its empire. (We await with interest the outcome

29

of Estonia's "radical" demands for economic independence and political freedom, and the stirrings in Eastern Europe.)

Within the Soviet bloc the Brezhnev Doctrine defines self-determination. Outside the bloc, the Soviet doctrine of "national liberation movements" carries the claim that it is *legitimate* to offer weapons and other support to a "national liberation struggle" against a nonsocialist state. Moscow often describes force in support of Marxist "liberation movements" as counterforce. The point here, however, is the claim that it is *legitimate* for the USSR to use force and the threat of force to assist Marxist struggles. As one Soviet international lawyer put it in a standard text on the subject: "Peaceful coexistence means abstention from armed force in relations between states so long as wars of national liberation and the struggle against aggression and colonialism are not involved."[13]

Thus, the Charter's provision that all states have the right to be free from the use or threat of force against their territorial integrity or political independence is redefined to maintain the independence of Soviet bloc countries and make it open season on any government that can be described as "alien, colonialist or racist."[14] In principle, any non-Soviet regime can be so described.

U.S. AND SOVIET POSITIONS: "MORAL" OR "LEGAL" EQUIVALENTS?

Some observers have argued that the Reagan Doctrine makes the United States and the Soviet Union equal offenders against the Charter's requirement of nonuse of force and noninterference in the internal affairs of others. They cite Hans Morgenthau's position that "the nationalistic universalism of our age claims for one nation and one state the right to impose its own valuations and standards of action upon all the other nations."[15] But surely Morgenthau never would have drawn a parallel between the nationalistic universalism of the Soviet Union and that of the United States. He would have known better than to argue that the United States "in appropriating the methods and rationalizations of the Soviet Union [in the Reagan Doctrine] runs a far greater risk today of taking on the cloak and imitating the values of its rival."[16]

To adopt the latter approach, which is shared by many critics of the Reagan Doctrine, is to err on several counts. First, it misunderstands the nature of the values that have traditionally guided the conduct of U.S. foreign policy. Second, it confuses the means the United States uses to transmit those values with the Soviets' mode of imposing their own values and standards of action upon other nations. Third, it misconstrues international law and the law of the UN Charter. That law, while honoring sovereign equality, prefers governments that permit freedom and democracy. Like all law worthy of the name, it is based on reciprocity. Finally, those who argue moral equivalence fail to understand that the application of the Reagan Doctrine in fact has decreased rather than enhanced the prospects of war with our major adversary, the Soviet Union.

The charge that the Reagan Doctrine comes close to being interchangeable with the Soviet doctrine of national liberation is baseless. The latter countenances *expansion* of Soviet power. The Reagan Doctrine permits assistance in self-defense. The Brezhnev Doctrine preserves foreign influence. The Reagan Doctrine restores self-government. It countenances counter-intervention, not intervention. The Reagan Doctrine is not a "roll-back," but it is a cousin to that idea.

These are not mere differences in words; they are important differences in meaning. Like the Truman Doctrine, the Reagan Doctrine permits counterforce and counterintervention only as a last resort if an independent government is thought to be under an attack that cannot be repelled by other means. The desirable norm is a world of sovereign states in which the principle of *democratic* self-determination is respected. Where that principle is forcibly suppressed through the assistance of an outside power, the United States reserves to itself the right to aid in its expression.

31

International law does not proscribe assistance in any and all circumstances to indigenous groups fighting for democratic self-determination. It prohibits aggression in international relations, a principle to which all American administrations have expressed fidelity.

Article 51 of the UN Charter provides for individual and collective self-defense in the case of an "armed attack." Furthermore, the protection of "territorial integrity" provided in article 2(4) is not the same thing as territorial inviolability. Territorial integrity is preserved so long as none of a state's territory is taken from it. Running throughout the Charter are two other themes, one explicit, the other implicit. The explicit theme, which appears from the Charter's statement of purposes and principles, is that human rights and individual freedoms, including the right of self-determination, are to be furthered. The implicit theme, stated by Ambassador Arthur J. Goldberg in testimony before Congress in 1965, is that either the same rules (at the time pertaining to collective financial responsibility) apply to all, or they apply to none. "There can be no double standard among the members of the organization," he stated.[17]

It is no secret that in the past the Soviets have made it their policy, as well as their doctrine, to intervene, with their own troops if deemed necessary, to enforce socialist solidarity and to overthrow "colonialist, racist, and alien regimes," which are, of course, always defined as nonsocialist states. To be sure, they at the same time have initiated or spurred consideration of various UN declarations—including the 1970 General Assembly Declaration on Principles of International Law concerning Friendly Relations and Co-operation among States in Accordance with the Charter of the United Nations[18]—that make it intolerable for states to foment subversion aimed at the violent overthrow of a regime, or to forcibly deny the free exercise of the right of self-determination. Moscow's actions, however, belie its words of sponsorship or participation in contradictory resolutions. Clearly, in the Soviets' version of things, they are free to intervene to support national liberation struggles against pro-Western regimes, while the United States, as they would have it, is denied a reciprocal right. But, as John Stuart Mill said more than one hundred years ago, "intervention to enforce non-intervention is always rightful, always moral, if not always prudent."

There is another aspect to this matter. The Soviets intervene to deny the free expression of self-determination: the only choice a people has is a variation upon the theme of socialism and one-party rule. The United States counterintervenes to preserve and promote freedom.

Some would argue, with good reason, that intervention on behalf of freedom should not be reserved for counterintervention. Kant suggested that for perpetual peace to be established, "the civil constitution in each state should be republican."[19] The law of nations had, Kant wrote, to be based on the freedom and the "moral integrity" of each nation. In Kant's view, intervention to bring down despotic governments was to be encouraged. The Reagan Doctrine does not go this far, but it has the same philosophical underpinnings. These underpinnings are, moreover, consonant with those of the UN Charter that encourage the promotion of human rights, liberties, and self-determination of peoples. The notion that the principle of sovereign equality precludes assistance to groups fighting for democratic self-determination against regimes dependent on the support of external powers is at odds with both the words of the UN Charter and state practice as it has evolved in the more than four decades since the Charter's adoption.

CONCLUSION

We have attempted to show that certain beliefs did not die with the signing of the UN Charter in 1945:

- Soviet leaders did not give up either the conviction that socialism is the appropriate (and inevitable) form of government for all peoples or the commitment to promote socialism in other countries—through national liberation movements, propaganda, disinformation, and, at times, direct use of force.

- American leaders did not abandon the conviction that legitimate government is based on respect for individual rights and the consent of the governed or the belief that all people deserve such government.

- The United Nations Charter is not neutral between these conceptions. It is committed to democratic values and practices. Where one state uses armed force or economic and military assistance to aid in the suppression of democratic values and practices, other states are free to act to redress the balance and stop the forcible repression of these values.

The majority vote of member-states of the UN General Assembly—which are predominantly nondemocratic—cannot deprive the United States or other democratic nations of this right. Moreover, the authority of the International Court of Justice requires that the court be more than an expression of the will of the concurrent majorities of the Security Council and the General Assembly, by which its judges are elected. The Charter does not require that the United States stand idly by while the Soviet Union assists in the suppression of liberties in countries with strong indigenous movements struggling against suppression. This interpretation of the Charter is supported by the American understanding at the time of its promulgation, and by the statements and actions of every U.S. administration since its adoption. The Reagan Doctrine articulates for our times the legal and moral basis for the historic American response.

Ironically, the articulation of the Reagan Doctrine is nearly as offensive to its opponents as its implementation is. Most opponents of the doctrine attack the notion that U.S. use of counterforce in support of democratic self-determination is *legitimate* rather than argue about the prudence of support for this or that insurgency. The idea that American power can be usefully and morally utilized in support of a world of independent, self-governing nations still seems implausible to those who define an appropriate world role for the United States in the shadow of their interpretation of the Vietnam War.

NOTES

1. John Stuart Mill, *Dissertations and Discussions: Political Philosophical and Historical*, vol. 3 (London, 1875), 176. Reprinted from Mill, "A Few Words on Non-Intervention," *Fraser's Magazine* (December 1859).
2. "Remarks at a Joint German-American Military Ceremony at Bitburg Air Base in the Federal Republic of Germany, May 5, 1985," *Public Papers of the Presidents of the United States: Ronald Reagan, 1985*, Book I (Washington, D.C.: U.S. Government Printing Office, 1988), p. 567.
3. "Address Before a Joint Session of the Congress on the State of the Union, February 6, 1985," *Public Papers of the Presidents of the United States: Ronald Reagan, 1985*, Book I (Washington, D.C.: U.S. Government Printing Office, 1988), p. 135.
4. See Michael Charlton, *The Eagle & the Small Birds* (Chicago: University of Chicago Press, 1985), p. 34.
5. "Special Message to the Congress on Greece and Turkey: The Truman Doctrine, March 12, 1947," *Public Papers of the Presidents of the United States: Harry S. Truman, 1947* (Washington, D.C.: U.S. Government Printing Office, 1963), pp. 178–79.
6. "Proclamation 3504: Interdiction of the Delivery of Offensive Weapons to Cuba, October 23, 1962," *Public Papers of the Presidents of the United States: John F. Kennedy, 1962* (Washington, D.C.: U.S. Government Printing Office, 1963), pp. 809–10.
7. Statement of May 1, 1965, *Department of State Bulletin* (Washington, D.C.: U.S. Government Printing Office, May 17, 1965), pp. 743–44.
8. D.D. Eisenhower, *Mandate for Change, 1953–1956* (New York: Doubleday, 1963), pp. 357 and 370–71.
9. Statement by Undersecretary of State for Political Affairs Bedell Smith, July 21, 1954. Quoted in U.S. Senate Committee on Foreign Relations, *Background Information Relating to Southeast Asia and Vietnam*, 3rd rev. ed. (Washington, D.C., 1967), p. 83.
10. Address of April 22, 1968, *Department of State Bulletin* (Washington, D.C.: U.S. Government Printing Office, May 13, 1968), pp. 605–607.
11. Statement at Third All-Russian Congress of Soviets, January 1918. Quoted in E.H. Carr, *The Bolshevik Revolution 1917–1923*, vol. 1 (Harmondsworth: Penguin Books, 1966), p. 272.
12. S. Kovalev, "Sovereignty and the International Obligations of Socialist Countries," *Pravda*, September 26, 1968. Quoted in *Current Digest of the Soviet Press*, vol. 20, no. 39 (1968), pp. 10–12.
13. F.I. Kozhevnikov, ed., *International Law* (Moscow: Foreign Languages Publishing House, 1964). Cited in B.A. Ramundo, *Peaceful Coexistence: International Law in the Building of Communism* (Baltimore: Johns Hopkins University Press, 1967), p. 116.
14. See, for example, United Nations General Assembly Resolution 36/171, December 16, 1981, in which the Soviet Union joined with a majority of other nations to condemn the U.S. legal system for the extradition to Israel of Abu Eain, a Palestinian fugitive, upon Israel's showing of probable cause to try him for murder of civilians resulting from the planting of a bomb

near a sports stadium in Tiberias. By a vote of seventy-five in favor to twenty-one against, with forty-three abstentions, the General Assembly ruled that even if the charges against him were true, the crime itself was not an offense, since "all available means"—including terrorism—may be employed in the struggle for "liberation from colonial and foreign domination and alien subjugation." See also General Assembly Resolution 40/61, December 9, 1985, on "measures to prevent international terrorism." This resolution, sponsored by Syria and Cuba, joined by the Soviet Union, condemned as criminal "all acts, methods and practices of terrorism wherever and by whomever committed," but also reaffirmed "the inalienable right to self-determination and independence of all peoples under colonial and racist regimes and other forms of alien domination, and upholding the legitimacy of their struggle, in particular the struggle of national liberation movements."

15. Hans J. Morgenthau, *Politics among Nations,* 6th ed., rev. by Kenneth W. Thompson (New York: Alfred A. Knopf, 1985), p. 351.
16. Kenneth W. Thompson, "Commentary: The Reagan Doctrine," in Robert W. Tucker, ed., *Intervention & the Reagan Doctrine* (New York: Council on Religion and International Affairs, 1985), p. 30.
17. Quoted in *U.S. Participation in the United Nations, Report by the President to the Congress for the Year 1965* (Washington, D.C.: U.S. Government Printing Office, 1967), p. 108.
18. United Nations General Assembly Resolution 2625 (25), October 24, 1970.
19. Immanuel Kant, "On Eternal Peace," trans. in Carl J. Friedrich, *Inevitable Peace* (Cambridge, MA: Harvard University Press, 1948), p. 250.

2

USE OF FORCE: LAW AND U.S. POLICY

Louis Henkin

In 1945, the Allied victors in the Second World War led some fifty nations in concluding the United Nations Charter, its principal purpose being to render the use of force between states unlawful and to end the scourge of war. Today, virtually every one of the world's 160 nations is party to the Charter and bound by its norms. Yet, in 1988, a terrible war between Iraq and Iran was in its eighth year. Another war had raged for eight years in nearby Afghanistan involving the USSR, one of the authors of the Charter. The United States, the principal architect of the law of the Charter, recently was found guilty of serious violations of international law by uses of force against Nicaragua.

Some might say they told us so. Even during the Charter honeymoon, respectable voices questioned the "legalistic-moralistic approach to international problems" that sought "to suppress the chaotic and dangerous aspirations of governments" by "legal rules and restraints."[1] Four decades later that skepticism is rampant. There is doubt if not cynicism as to the efficacy of law in deterring, preventing, or terminating the use of force, as to whether its prescriptions are relevant and material to the policies of nations. In the United States, some have asked why their country should attend to the law since others do not. Some have asked whether any law should limit the U.S. pursuit of its national interest as it sees it, by force if the government deems necessary. Even those who are committed to the law of the Charter admit that it is in some disarray. Important states disagree strongly as to what the law forbids in significant respects; clear violations of undisputed law continue.

What is the international law on the use of force today? How has that law fared? Can the law be improved and made more effective? What should the United States do about it?

THE LAW OF THE CHARTER

The UN Charter declared purposes and prescribed norms, and it laid down a blueprint for an organization that would pursue those purposes and enforce those norms. After more than forty years, all know, the organization is different from that contemplated: in particular, the Security Council has not been effective in enforcing the principles of the Charter outlawing the use of force, and efforts to have the General Assembly substitute for the Security Council have not been notably successful. But no responsible voice, surely no government, has suggested that the failures of the organization vitiated the agreement and nullified or modified the Charter's norms.[2] The Charter remains the authoritative statement of the law on the use of force. It is the principal norm of international law of this century.

The crucial norm is set forth in article 2(4). It provides as follows:

> All members shall refrain in their international relations from the threat or use of force against the territorial integrity or political independence of any state, or in any other manner inconsistent with the purposes of the United Nations.

The Charter reflected universal agreement that the status quo prevailing at the end of World War II was not to be changed by force. Even justified grievances and a sincere concern for "national security" or other "vital interests" would not warrant any nation's initiating war. Peace was the paramount value. The Charter and the organization were dedicated to realizing other values as well—self-determination, respect for human rights, economic and social development, justice, and a just international order. But those purposes could not justify the use of force between states to achieve them; they would have to be pursued by other means. Peace was more important than progress and more important than justice. The purposes of the United Nations could not in fact be achieved by war. War inflicted the greatest injustice, the most serious violations of human rights, and the most violence to self-determination and to economic and social development. War was inherently unjust. In the future, the only "just war" would be war against an aggressor—in self-defense by the victim, in collective defense of the victim by others, or by all. Nations would be assured independence, the undisturbed enjoyment of autonomy within their territory, and their right to be let alone. Change—other than internal change through internal forces—would have to be achieved peacefully by international agreement. Henceforth there would be order so that international society could concentrate on meeting better the needs of justice and human welfare.

Efforts to Reconstrue the Charter

During the early postwar years there was general agreement as to what the prescriptions of article 2(4) meant. Clearly, the article outlaws war and other acts of armed aggression by one state against another; it also forbids lesser forms of intervention by force by one state in the territory of another. Apart from collective action under the auspices of the United Nations to enforce the peace, the only lawful use of force by a state is that contemplated under the limited exception in article 51 permitting the use of force in self-defense against an armed attack. In time, the language of article 2(4) proved to be not without ambiguities and not invulnerable to claims that intervention by force is permitted for certain "benign" purposes.

One initial ambiguity appears on the face of article 2(4). Does the prohibition of the use of force against "the territorial integrity" of another state forbid only a use of force designed to deprive that state of territory, or does it also prohibit force that violates the territorial borders of that state, however temporarily and for whatever purpose? Does the prohibition of the use of force against "the political independence" of another state outlaw only a use of force that aims to end that state's political independence by annexing it or rendering it a puppet, or does it also prohibit force designed to coerce that state to follow a particular policy or take a particular decision? In what other circumstances would a use or threat of force be "inconsistent with the purposes of the United Nations"? Another debate concerned whether economic pressure—an oil embargo, a boycott, or other sanctions—designed to derogate from a state's territorial integrity or political independence is a "use of force" prohibited by article 2(4).

An effective United Nations system, or a court with comprehensive jurisdiction and recognized authority, might have answered these and other questions by developing the law of the Charter through construction and case-by-case application. In the absence of such authoritative interpretation, the meaning of the Charter has been shaped by the actions and reactions of states and by the opinions of publicists and scholars. Scholars have debated the ambiguities of the Charter that I have cited and other questions of interpretation; a government occasionally has sought to shape the law to justify an action it has taken. But governments generally have insisted on the interpretations most restrictive of the use of force: the Charter outlaws war for any reason; it prohibits the use of armed force by one state on the territory of another or against the forces, vessels, or other public property of another state located anywhere, for any purpose, in any circumstances. Virtually every use of force in the years since the Charter was signed has been clearly condemned by virtually all states. Virtually every putative justification of a use of force has been rejected. Over the years since the Charter's adoption, even states that have perpetrated acts of force, when seeking to justify their acts, have not commonly urged a relaxed interpretation of the prohibition. Rather, they have asserted facts and circumstances that might have rendered their actions not unlawful. For example, in 1950, North Korea claimed that the South Korean army had initiated hostilities, permitting North Korea to act in self-defense; in Czechoslovakia in 1948 and 1968, and in Hungary in 1956, the USSR claimed that its troops had been invited by the legitimate authorities to help preserve order.

Indeed, the community of states has acted formally to tighten the Charter's restrictions. The Declaration on Principles of International Law concerning Friendly Relations and Co-operation among States in Accordance with the Charter of the United Nations, adopted by consensus in the General Assembly in 1970, and the Definition of Aggression, adopted by consensus in 1974, have restated and expanded the law of the Charter as prohibiting armed intervention and aggression, broadly conceived.[3] The resolution defining aggression made it clear that prohibited forms of aggression include not only invasion, but also attack or military occupation, however temporary; sending armed bands or mercenaries that carry out grave acts of armed force;[4] bombarding a state's territory; blocking its ports; and attacking the forces of another state (wherever they are).

Suggested Exceptions to the Prohibitions of Article 2(4)

In time, however, some states claimed exceptions to the absolute prohibitions of article 2(4), as permitting intervention by force for certain "benign" purposes (in addition to the self-defense exception under article 51). None of the "benign exceptions" has been formally accepted; only one has brought wide acquiescence.

Humanitarian intervention. On several occasions states have claimed the right to use force in "humanitarian intervention." The paradigmatic case was the action of Israel in 1976 to extricate hostages held on a hijacked plane at Entebbe (Uganda). The United States claimed its unsuccessful attempt in 1980 to liberate the diplomatic hostages held in Teheran also came within the exception. States have been reluctant to adopt this exception to article 2(4) formally, but the legal community has widely accepted that the Charter does not prohibit humanitarian intervention by use of force strictly limited to what is necessary to save lives.

The exception, I believe, is not restricted to actions by a state on behalf of its own nationals. But it is a right to liberate hostages

41

if the territorial state cannot or will not do so. It has not been accepted, however, that a state has a right to intervene by force to topple a government or occupy its territory even if that were necessary to terminate atrocities or to liberate detainees. Entebbe was acceptable, but the occupation of Cambodia by Vietnam was not.[5] The U.S. invasion and occupation of Grenada, even if in fact designed to protect the lives of U.S. nationals, also was widely challenged.[6]

Intervention to support self-determination. The suggestion that a state may intervene by force to help a people achieve "self-determination" in some circumstances has received some support.

Self-determination is a powerful political dogma that has been accepted as a principle of international law. It is incorporated in widely accepted treaties, including both the International Covenant on Civil and Political Rights and the International Covenant on Economic, Social and Cultural Rights. The concept of self-determination cries for definition, and few agree on its content, but all agree that it includes at least the right of peoples in Asia and Africa to be free from colonial domination, Western style.

Neither article 2(4) of the Charter nor any other provision of international law forbids authentic revolution and wars of independence. Indeed, there is a strong case that it is now unlawful for a state to maintain an unwilling people in colonial status, and such unlawfulness is compounded if a colony is maintained by force. A very different question, however, is whether an external power is permitted to intervene by force to help expel the colonial power or hasten its departure.

On various theories, many states have supported the right to intervene by force to help an entity achieve independence from colonial rule.[7] The United States has firmly rejected any such right. In addressing India's invasion and occupation of Goa (Portuguese India) in 1961, Ambassador Adlai Stevenson said:

> What is at stake today is not colonialism; it is a bold violation of one of the most basic principles in the United Nations Charter. . . . But

if our Charter means anything, it means that states are obligated to renounce the use of force, are obligated to seek a solution of their differences by peaceful means.[8]

India used force to end Portuguese control in Goa and claimed the territory for itself; later, other states asserted a general right to intervene by force to help a people achieve independence. In a famous statement, attributed to Leonid Brezhnev, defending the Soviet invasion of Czechoslovakia in 1968, the USSR decried those who "regard the notion of sovereignty as prohibiting support for the struggle of progressive forces." He added: "Genuine revolutionaries, being internationalists, cannot but support progressive forces in their just struggle for national and social liberation."[9]

The world rejected Brezhnev's invasion of Czechoslovakia; even the Third World was not persuaded by the "national liberation" justification. General Assembly resolutions, however, have confirmed the right of colonial peoples to achieve independence by force if necessary and included ambiguous declarations that suggested a right of other states to intervene to help them.[10]

With colonialism no longer an important concern, the pressure for a "self-determination exception" to the law of the Charter has subsided, and the potential significance of such an exception, if recognized, is sharply reduced.

Intervention for socialism: The Brezhnev Doctrine. The Brezhnev regime also asserted generally the right of any socialist state to intervene in another when socialism there is threatened. It said:

> Just as, in Lenin's words, a man living in a society cannot be free from the society, a particular socialist state, staying in a system of other states composing the socialist community, cannot be free from the common interests of that community.
>
> The sovereignty of each socialist country cannot be opposed to the interests of the world of socialism, of the world revolutionary movement. . . .
>
> Discharging their internationalist duty toward the fraternal peoples of Czechoslovakia and defending their own socialist gains, the U.S.S.R. and the other socialist states had to act decisively and they did act against the antisocialist forces in Czechoslovakia.[11]

The Brezhnev Doctrine has been generally condemned. The USSR itself appears to have disavowed it in the Helsinki accords.[12]

Intervention for democracy. Self-determination as a justification for the use of force to end colonialism has lost its raison d'être, but some have invoked a people's right to "internal self-determination" to support the use of force by one state to preserve or impose democracy in another. One suggestion, for example, is that article 2(4) permits the use of force to "enhance opportunities of ongoing self-determination . . . to increase the probability of the free choice of peoples about their government and political structure."[13] Some see this view as the foundation of the so-called Reagan Doctrine, construed as including a claim of the right to intervene by force in another state to preserve or impose democracy.

The claim has received no support by any other government. Like the use of force to impose or maintain socialism or any other ideology, the use of force for democracy clearly would be contrary to the language of article 2(4), to the intent of its framers, and to the construction long given to that article by the United States.[14]

At bottom, all suggestions for exceptions to article 2(4) imply that, contrary to the assumptions of the Charter's framers, there are universally recognized values higher than peace and the autonomy of states. In general, the claims of peace and state autonomy have prevailed.[15]

Self-defense under the Charter

Serious issues about the meaning of the law of the Charter have revolved around the right of self-defense.

The UN Charter makes an explicit exception to article 2(4). Article 51 provides:

> Nothing in the present Charter shall impair the inherent right of individual or collective self-defence if an armed attack occurs against a Member of the United Nations, until the Security Council

has taken measures necessary to maintain international peace and security.[16]

The original intent of article 51 seems clear: despite the prohibition on the unilateral use of force in article 2(4), a victim of an armed attack may use force to defend itself, and others may join to use force in collective self-defense of the victim, pending action by the Security Council. No one has doubted that the right of individual or collective self-defense against armed attack continues to apply if the Security Council does not act, or if—as later proved to be the case—the Security Council becomes generally incapable of acting.[17] It has also been accepted that the right of self-defense, individual or collective, is subject to limitations of "necessity" and "proportionality," but that self-defense includes a right both to repel the armed attack and to take the war to the aggressor state in order effectively to terminate the attack and prevent a recurrence. It is generally accepted, too, that states are permitted to organize themselves in advance in bona fide collective self-defense arrangements (such as the North Atlantic Treaty Organization) for possible response if one of the members should become the victim of an armed attack.

The right of self-defense is available "if an armed attack occurs." In the wake of Suez-Sinai (1956), however, some publicists began to argue that the "inherent right of self-defense" recognized by article 51 is the traditional right of self-defense, predating the Charter, which was not limited to defense against "armed attack." They argued that the right of self-defense "if an armed attack occurs" does not mean "only if an armed attack occurs." The only limitation on self-defense, they said, was that implied in the famous *Caroline* dictum: that the right of self-defense was available only when "the necessity of that self-defence is instant, overwhelming, and leaving no choice of means, and no moment for deliberation."[18]

This more permissive interpretation of article 51 found favor with some commentators, but little with governments. The United States rejected it when its allies in effect invoked it at Suez (1956). During the Cuban missile crisis (1962), the United States, though eager to justify its blockade of Cuba, pointedly refrained from adopting the "loose" construction of article 51 and did not claim as justification a right to act in "inherent self-defense."[19] To this day, the United States has not claimed a right to act in self-defense where no armed attack has occurred. In 1985, however, the United States interpreted the concept of armed attack to include certain terrorist activities. Declaring the Libyan government responsible for terrorist acts in Europe, including the bombing of a Berlin nightclub frequented by U.S. servicemen in which one was killed and many wounded, the United States launched a bomb attack on targets in Libyan territory. President Reagan described the attack as "fully consistent with Article 51 of the UN Charter," presumably because, in the American view, the terrorist act was an "armed attack" justifying the bombing as a use of force in self-defense.

In that case, the United States also referred to its attack as a "preemptive action." The legal implication of that phrase was not elaborated. Publicists have debated whether, under article 51, a state may use force in "preemptive," or "anticipatory," self-defense, particularly in the context of nuclear strategy. Some have suggested that if a state has strong reasons to believe it is about to be the target of a nuclear strike, the "armed attack has occurred" and the victim need not wait but may "respond" in "anticipatory self-defense." Fortunately, that issue has remained academic. The justification for the attack on Libya, however, apparently was using "preemptive action" in a different sense. The action was not designed to "beat Libya to the punch," but, President Reagan said, it "will not only diminish Colonel Quadhafi's capacity to export terror, it will provide him with incentives and reasons to alter his criminal behavior."[20]

The bombing of Libya by the United States was widely condemned and the claimed justification widely rejected.[21]

Intervention and Counterintervention

Before the UN Charter, the law seemed to be that a state may provide military assistance to the government of another state, even to help it suppress rebellion, but a state could not assist

46

rebels against the incumbent government of another state. If rebellion succeeded sufficiently to achieve the status of "belligerent" and constitute a civil war, the law probably forbade assistance to either side. That law, confirmed by special Non-Intervention Agreements in the 1930s, was battered during the Spanish Civil War as states intervened on both sides. The United States, however, honored the principle of nonintervention, helping neither side.

The United Nations Charter did not expressly address intervention in civil wars. Nothing in article 2(4) forbids sending military assistance to an incumbent government, but the use of force in support of rebels against an incumbent government would be a use of force against the territorial integrity of the state and, presumably, against its political independence. Under the Charter, a state probably may not send troops into the territory of another state to support either side in a civil war, since that too would violate the latter's territorial integrity and compromise its political independence. Assistance not involving the use of force, however—for example, providing advice, selling arms, or giving financial assistance to one (or both) sides in a civil war—seems not to be covered by article 2(4), but may violate norms against nonintervention that predate the Charter and have been strongly restated in numerous General Assembly resolutions.

Authoritative Construction of the Law: The Nicaragua Case

States that have used force have sometimes construed the law so as to justify their actions or have defended against charges of violation by denying or distorting the facts or mischaracterizing the circumstances. States generally have condemned virtually every use of force in the decades since World War II. Explicitly or by implication they have adopted a most restrictive view of the Charter's law on the use of force. Recently the restrictive construction received authoritative support in major respects.

In 1986, in the *Nicaragua* case, the International Court of Justice issued what is in effect its first judgment construing key elements in the law of the Charter.[22] It construed the prohibition in article 2(4) broadly (as imposing strict limitations on the use of force) and the exception in article 51 narrowly (as limiting the circumstances in which force may be used in self-defense). In effect, it rejected both the Brezhnev Doctrine and the Reagan Doctrine. It also rejected the "Suez interpretation" of article 51.

In a long, wide-ranging, and far-reaching opinion,[23] the court held (or said) the following:

- The only exception to article 2(4) is article 51: Force against another state that is not justified by a right of self-defense under Article 51 is in violation of Article 2(4) (paragraph 211).

- Whether self-defense is individual or collective, "the exercise of this right is subject to the State concerned having been the victim of an armed attack" (paragraphs 195, 232).

- Armed attack may include acts by armed bands where such acts occur on a significant scale, but "assistance to rebels in the form of the provision of weapons or logistical or other support is not an armed attack justifying the use of force in self-defense" (paragraph 195).

- A state may use force in "collective self-defense" in support of another only if the victim state has declared itself to have been the object of an armed attack and has requested assistance in collective self-defense (paragraphs 195–99).

- "States do not have a right of 'collective' armed response to acts which do not constitute an 'armed attack' " (paragraphs 210–11). If no armed attack has occurred, collective self-defense is unlawful, even if "carried on in strict compliance with the canons of necessity and proportionality" (paragraph 237).

- The court could not "contemplate the creation of a new rule opening up a right of intervention by one State against another on the ground that the latter has opted for some particular ideology or political system." And "to hold otherwise would make nonsense of the fundamental principle of State sovereignty, on which the whole of international law rests, and the freedom of choice of the political, social, economic and cultural system of a State" (paragraph 263).

- There is no "general right of intervention, in support of an opposition within another state" (paragraph 209).
- The "use of force could not be the appropriate method to monitor or ensure" respect for human rights (paragraph 268).

The court did not resolve important questions as to the law of the Charter. In particular, the *Nicaragua* judgment gave only partial guidance on the difficult issues of intervention and counterintervention. The court denied any right to intervene by force in another state for purposes other than collective self-defense against armed attack; it denied any right to use force against another state in response to the latter's intervention in a third state by means that do not constitute an armed attack. But the court did not address the victim's right of armed response to "less than an armed attack," or what means other than force can be used in response to such interventions by either the victim or its friends (see paragraph 210). The court did not address whether when a state supports one side in a civil war in another country, a third state may "counterintervene" on the other side and, if so, subject to what limitations.

The *Nicaragua* case did not bring other current issues in the law of the Charter before the court. Thus, the court did not decide whether a target state (and its allies) may use force in anticipation of an armed attack (see paragraph 194). Its opinion gives no guidance as to whether a state responsible for terrorist activities may have committed an armed attack either against the state in whose territory such activities took place or against a state whose nationals were the targets or the victims of those activities.

A decision of the International Court of Justice is not binding on states other than the parties to the case, but judicial decisions are "subsidiary means for the determination of rules of law" (article 38 of the Statute of the Court), and decisions of the court are highly authoritative. The court's principal conclusions, representing the views of an overwhelming majority of the judges,[24] will doubtless be accepted by states generally and by the large majority of the legal community both in the United States and elsewhere.

The court's opinion is not the last word. The Reagan administration in the United States may not have been alone in rejecting some of its implications. But it is important to sort out the different conclusions. The court's declaration that force may be used only in self-defense against an armed attack reaffirms the original intent of the Charter and the positions commonly held by states (other than the few that have sought to justify their own uses of force). Extravagant claims of right to act in self-defense have been the principal threat to the law of the Charter. The court's construction of the Charter is more likely to achieve its purposes and maintain international peace and security.

Less clear, more likely to be reexamined, and requiring much refinement are the court's definition of "armed attack" and its statement of the law as to what is permitted to a victim state (**and** its friends) in response to violations that do not constitute an armed attack. These—and other issues of intervention and counterintervention—are the legal agenda for the years ahead.

THE LAW OF THE CHARTER AND THE BEHAVIOR OF STATES

In principle, and in formal acts and pronouncements of states, the international system has maintained its commitment to the rule of the law of the Charter. It has insisted on the law and often has acted formally to condemn violations.[25] But clearly the international system has not been sufficiently effective to deter, prevent, or terminate important violations. The Security Council was frustrated by big-power division. The General Assembly did not effectively assume the council's role.

The Charter's law has been violated, but not as frequently as is commonly assumed. In the decades since the Charter's adoption, the world has seen few wars between states of the kind it knew earlier in this century—the two World Wars, the Japanese conquest of Manchuria, Italy's conquest of Ethiopia, and the long Gran Chaco War in Latin America. No wars have occurred either among the major powers, in Europe, or within the Western Hemisphere.[26] But several Arab-Israeli wars have taken place, as have an invasion of South Korea, more recently Iraq's attack on Iran, and the Falklands War. And flurries of hostilities have erupted—between India and Pakistan, Greece and Turkey (over Cyprus), Libya and Egypt, Cambodia and Thailand, Vietnam and Cambodia, India and China, Ethiopia and Somalia.

In the main, hostilities in our times have taken the form of "interventions" and "counterinterventions." From the lawyer's perspective, some of these have been cases of "indirect aggression"—notably those involving the USSR in Czechoslovakia (twice), in Hungary, and more recently in Afghanistan. Some have been cases of support for rebels against incumbent governments, sometimes followed by "counterintervention" by other states—in Vietnam, El Salvador, Nicaragua, Chad, and Angola, among others. All probably involved some violations of international law, even if not always of article 2(4). Terrorism has spread its own terrors and has occasionally evoked uses of force by states on the territory of other states, as when the United States dropped bombs in Libya or when Israel attacks targets in Lebanon linked to the Palestine Liberation Organization. The inadequacies of the system to deter, prevent, or terminate unlawful uses of force, dramatized by the failures of the United Nations, reflect inadequate commitment by influential states and divisive world political forces. Whether in cold war or détente, the conflict between East and West sometimes has taken forms involving violations of the Charter. The USSR has insisted on maintaining its control in Eastern Europe, by force if necessary; it has not refrained from seeking to extend its influence elsewhere, sometimes by force. The United States has been determined to resist communist expansion, particularly penetration of the Western Hemisphere, and sometimes has succumbed to the temptation to act without regard to the law of the Charter. East-West conflict has ideological undertones that have invited or can be exploited for external interventions in various countries, sometimes in covert or ambiguous forms that are not readily amenable to legal determinations and judgments, and are not readily deterred or terminated.

Conflict and competition between the big powers has weakened also their willingness and ability to help keep the peace generally. The many poor, less-developed states are generally less content with the status quo. Some do not share a paramount commitment to peace and order. A few have their particular grievances against neighbors and their own ambitions. Ideological-political conflict among the big powers has led to the concept and the implications of the "Third World" and to "nonalignment," which give Third World states some immunity from big power objection or Security Council condemnation. Their solidarity also gives Third World states substantial immunity from adverse community judgment in the UN General Assembly. Arab-Israeli wars and recurrent hostilities, the Iran-Iraq War, wars and interventions in Southeast Asia and on the Asian subcontinent, hostilities involving Ethiopia or Libya, and others have not had to take serious account of the law or of judgment by the political community.

The law is not in robust condition, but few would suggest that it is moribund. The political system remains committed to it in principle. Violations of the law have not been sufficient to destroy it, the institutions that work with it, or states' commitment to it. The influence of law is difficult to identify and assess, but the law, operating within the political processes of the international system, has helped deter, prevent, or terminate some wars and continues to provide strong support to forces opposing the use of force.

THE LAW OF THE CHARTER
AND U.S. FOREIGN POLICY

Until recently, the United States was, and was generally recognized to be, a principal champion of the law of the Charter, insisting on its validity and on its interpretation to limit strictly the permissible uses of force. The United States condemned the use of force wherever it appeared and whatever state resorted to it. In 1948, and later, it condemned the use of force by Arab states against Israel. In 1950, the United States led the United

Nations into war against aggression by North Korea. At Suez, in 1956, the United States condemned the use of force by its principal allies. It inveighed against "indirect aggression" in Czechoslovakia in 1948, in Hungary in 1956, and again in Czechoslovakia in 1968. The United States flatly rejected the Brezhnev Doctrine as a clear violation of the Charter. In 1980, it led the condemnation of the Soviet invasion of Afghanistan. For decades the United States was a voice for self-restraint against uses of force and for law and international order.

For its own part, the United States had a good record of compliance with the law of the Charter. In general, it refrained from the use of force even in circumstances in which, in earlier times, that might have been a serious option. Nevertheless, the United States committed violations of the Charter. Other states, and many lawyers (including some in the United States), condemned it for the Bay of Pigs (1961), for sending troops to the Dominican Republic (1965), for its believed role in toppling governments in Guatemala (1957) and Chile (1973), and for its intervention in Vietnam. Like other states, the United States has not pleaded guilty to any violations, and it has not been as adept as, say, the USSR in concealing or distorting facts. However, in order to justify its actions it has sometimes characterized complex situations in ways that the community has not accepted.[27] But the United States did not preach what it may have practiced; it did not seek to reinterpret the law of the Charter so as to weaken its restraints. In sum, there were no compelling grounds for questioning the commitment of the United States to the law forbidding the use of force.

In recent years, the U.S. commitment to the law of the Charter has come into serious question, principally because of an array of actions the United States has taken and of the justifications it has claimed for them.[28] In a number of cases the justifications depended on assertions that the United States has not sought to prove and that have not been widely accepted. In some respects the United States also has reconstrued the law of the Charter in ways that the world—and lawyers, including most lawyers in the United States—have rejected.

The United States has recently claimed the right to use force against the territorial integrity and political independence of another state on a number of grounds and in various circumstances.

- In 1983, the United States invaded Grenada. The invasion was variously justified—as necessary to save lives of U.S. nationals; as responding to an invitation by the governor-general; as urged by Grenada's small neighbors; as required to restore to the people the right of self-determination and democracy. The alleged grounds have been widely challenged as spurious or as not justifying the action.

- The United States bombed Libya, which it held responsible for acts of terrorism, one of which had led to the death of a number of U.S. servicemen. Libya's responsibility for the particular terrorist attack was later questioned; the legal justification—self-defense against "armed attack" in addition to "preemption"—was widely rejected.

- The United States mined Nicaraguan harbors and supported rebellion by the contras. It claimed that its actions were legally justified on the ground that Nicaragua was guilty of aggression against El Salvador and that the United States was acting in collective self-defense with El Salvador. Many, including numerous members of Congress, questioned the U.S. version, interpretation, and characterization of the facts. The International Court of Justice, several governments, and most lawyers (including, it appeared, most American lawyers) rejected justifications claimed by the United States.

It is commonly accepted that U.S. action in Grenada and support for the contras are manifestations of the "Reagan Doctrine."[29] The Reagan administration never formally declared any such doctrine, and the term is used variously and loosely by both champions and opponents. A "Reagan policy" is reflected in actions, justifications, and official and unofficial but authoritative statements, by which the United States seems to have claimed the right generally to use force to impose and restore "democracy," particularly where communism exists or threatens. Virtually all who have considered such a policy—including, in effect, the International Court of Justice—have rejected it.

Given all its actions and justifications, the United States appears to have adopted the view that under international law a state may use force in and against another country for the following reasons:

- to overthrow the government of that country in order to protect lives there;
- to counter intervention there by another state and carry the attack to the territory of the intervening state;
- to overthrow the government of that country on the ground that it is helping to undermine another friendly government;
- in reprisal for that country's suspected responsibility for terrorist activities and in the hope of deterring such acts in the future;
- to overthrow a communist (or "procommunist") government or to prevent a communist (or "procommunist") government from assuming power, even if it was popularly elected or emerged as a result of internal forces.

Such a "Reagan policy" should be distinguished, in my view, from earlier U.S. policy. The United States has been determined to "contain" the USSR since the beginning of the Cold War, shortly after the end of the Second World War. Presidents have expressed that determination in various forms, some of which have acquired labels, beginning with the Truman Doctrine. Earlier "doctrines" and "policies," however, were designed to be and were expressed in terms consistent with the law of the Charter. They announced that the United States would act in collective self-defense with governments resisting "armed attack" by the USSR or other communist-state forces, including "indirect aggression" supported by local bands. The United States, then, was asserting the right to defend democracy (and other forms of "noncommunism") against the spread of communism by force from the outside, whether by direct attack or by indirect aggression. There was no serious suggestion that the United States would, and had the right under international law to, intervene to "roll back" communism or to prevent "defection" to communism by overthrowing or forestalling a communist regime resulting from popular vote or otherwise installed by essentially local forces.[30] The "Reagan policy" seems to have claimed the right to intervene by force to prevent or remove such a regime.

Whatever its domestic appeal, the "Reagan policy" as commonly understood is untenable in law, and the United States cannot lawfully pursue it. It may be permissible to intervene by limited force strictly for the purpose of protecting and liberating hostages when the territorial state is unable or unwilling to protect or liberate them; it is not permissible to overthrow a government to that end—as Vietnam did in Cambodia, and the United States in Grenada. International law provides no more basis for permitting the export of democracy by force than for permitting the export of socialism by force. As a matter of law, one cannot justify the U.S. action in Grenada or support for the contras and condemn the Soviet Union's role in Czechoslovakia. None of these is within the spirit of the Charter as conceived or as the United States interpreted it during its first thirty-five years. Distinguishing between them as a matter of law is hopeless in a world where many of the 160 states claim to be socialist and few of them have authentic democracy. It is not permissible under the Charter to use force to impose or secure democracy; nor does the Charter contain a Monroe Doctrine exception that would permit the United States to use force to keep the Western Hemisphere free of communism. In the *Nicaragua* case, the International Court of Justice rejected the "Reagan policy," as it had the Brezhnev Doctrine. Its decision conforms to the views of most (almost all) states and most lawyers. Indeed, it conforms to the views that the U.S. government itself held until a few years ago. The United States might assert that it thinks the law is otherwise, but rejecting the majority view would not validate the new American view of the law and would not free the United States to act on its novel interpretation.

Issues for the New U.S. Administration

The law of the Charter has not been formally amended. States generally have essentially maintained the original meaning of the Charter, both in formal resolutions of international bodies and in individual statements, and the International Court of Justice has largely reaffirmed it. Publicists and scholars treat the law of the Charter as established and as clear in most respects. Uncertainties are mainly about "intervention" and "counterintervention." Ambiguities in its application are due principally to difficulties of determining, appraising, and characterizing facts in complex circumstances, notably of interventions and counterinterventions.

A new administration took office in 1989 with a legacy of recent U.S. actions involving the use of force that have been opposed by many in the United States and, in some instances, have been widely and authoritatively condemned as unlawful. The administration is not likely to reexamine abstract questions of law or theoretical questions about the significance of law in international relations. But attitudes toward international law[31] and particularly the law of the Charter will be implicated in issues of war and peace between particular states that will come into our diplomatic ken bilaterally or in the United Nations. Attitudes toward international law will be implicated when this administration formulates policies on containing communism and responding to terrorism.

Rejecting the Law

I dismiss extreme hypothetical options for the United States. In theory, the United States could decide that the law of the Charter has been a mistake; that it is not viable; that one cannot subject the decisions of governments on national security and vital interests to restraints by legal norms; that it is undesirable—indeed, dangerous—to pretend that there is law when in fact there is none. Or the United States might decide that if the law on the use of force is not as it wishes it to be, it would prefer no law on the subject. Or it might decide that the USSR has not in fact been restrained by law and that it is therefore not in U.S. interests to be so restrained.

Whatever some hard-nosed editorial writers may say,[32] scuttling the law of the Charter is not a viable policy for any U.S. government. Even if the United States were persuaded that the law is wholly futile and deceptive, it would not be in U.S. interests to scrap it and, with it, the fruits of the Second World War and the hopes, aspirations, and efforts of half a century. Rejecting the Charter in effect would reject Nuremberg, undermine our national justification in history, and reestablish Adolf Hitler as no worse than anyone else. Such a move would be condemned by the whole world.[33] It would serve no good for the United States. The end of the rule of the Charter's law would not encourage cooperation for other law we seek, such as to outlaw and deny haven to terrorists, or to solve international economic ills.

The law of the Charter is here to stay. For the years ahead the interpretation of that law that renders the prohibition on the use force most stringent is also here to stay.

Modifying the Law

The United States might say that if what it has claimed to be the law is not the law, then it ought to be; the government might then urge modification accordingly. The United States might insist that the desirable law is not only in its national interest but also in that of other states, notably the USSR, and that it reflects the real world. The desirable law would recognize that the United States and the USSR will continue to compete; that they have in fact accepted, and are entitled to maintain, if not spheres of influence, then "critical defense areas"—the Western Hemisphere and Eastern Europe, respectively—in which each power sees a vital interest and can maintain its "system" by force, including the right to "prevent defection" regardless of the wishes of local governments or peoples.

No such change in the law—surely no formal change—is likely. Nor would such a change be desirable. It is difficult to obtain agreement on a change in the law. Any modification that would relax prohibitions on the use of force would be particularly resisted. The nations of the world—even ones that have violated the Charter—are committed to it. The many small nations see it as the guarantee of their independence and autonomy. Law corresponding to the "Reagan policy" or to spheres of influence would be rejected out of hand. As applied to Latin America, it would be seen as a return to "Yankee imperialism" and a rejection of the sovereignty of twenty states.

Perhaps, over time, by actions and assertions, the United States could move and shape law informally to make it more permissive, even if so doing entailed eroding the rule of law and courting disorder and charges of violation along the way. In fact, it is not clear that the United States would wish to see that view of the law prevail generally. U.S. actions and justifications for them are not an indication that the United States would like to have all states legally free to do as it has done. The United States has asserted rights of intervention and counterintervention, but it has challenged the right of others (Libya, South Africa, Cuba, Syria, Iran, Israel) to follow policies that appear comparable under international law. In Grenada and in Nicaragua, the United States apparently has been asserting the right to use force to impose or restore democracy, but presumably it would continue to oppose a rule that would permit other states to use force to impose their version of democracy or another ideology (socialism).[34]

Like every country, the United States occasionally is disposed to interpret the Charter in accordance with its own interests as it sees them. But an interpretation that does not accord with text, purpose, design, history, and other accepted principles of treaty construction will persuade nobody and will serve no purpose. Moreover, an interpretation that may appeal to a particular constituency in the United States will not necessarily appeal to others. What will appeal at a particular time may not at a different time. What is popular is not necessarily what is in the interest of the United States. A construction of the law that may be in the immediate interest of the United States may not be in its longer, deeper interests.

It is not in the interest of the United States to reconstrue the law of the Charter so as to dilute and confuse its normative prohibitions. In our decentralized international political system with primitive institutions and underdeveloped law enforcement machinery, it is important that Charter norms—which go to the heart of international order and implicate war and peace in the nuclear age—be clear, sharp, and comprehensive; as independent as possible of judgments of degree and of issues of fact; as invulnerable as can be to self-serving interpretations and to temptations to conceal, distort, or mischaracterize events. Extending the meaning of "armed attack" and of "self-defense," multiplying exceptions to the prohibition on the use of force and the occasions that would permit military intervention, would undermine the law of the Charter and the international order established in the wake of world war.

A Legal Agenda for the Future

The United States can—and should—live with the law of the Charter as intended, as commonly construed, as determined by the International Court of Justice, and as the United States construed it in the past. Until a very few years ago, it lived very well with that law; even when tempted into questionable actions—Cuba, the Dominican Republic—it sought to contain such aberrations and maintain the Charter norm rather than reject or revise it. The recent deviations—Grenada, Libya, Nicaragua— were not inevitable or necessary, nor did they "succeed"; many observers are not persuaded that they served even a short-term, narrow national interest. The United States has discontinued mining of harbors and other activities against Nicaragua; military support to the contras generates little enthusiasm. Grenada afforded a small, brief infusion of national euphoria, but many are not persuaded that it was worth the various costs. There is no evidence that another Grenada will not be far more expensive and will be worth those higher costs. The new administration would do well to decide that U.S. interests lie not in generalizing those actions into continuing policy, but in turning its back on them as aberrational and recommitting the United States to a stricter view of the prohibitions on the use of force. This does not mean that the law requires us to give free rein to Soviet expansion. If it proves necessary, the United States should recommit itself to the Truman Doctrine: the United States is entitled to help secure democracy by assisting an incumbent democratic government against armed attack, direct and indirect, or even against threatened internal rebellion.

For the rest, the United States would be free to promote democracy and human rights around the world by example, by friendship, by economic and other assistance, but not by the use of force. Clearly, it was the original intent of the Charter to forbid the use of force even to promote human rights or to install authentic democracy. Nothing has happened to justify deviations from that commitment. Human rights are indeed violated in every country. In some countries violations are egregious. But the use of force remains itself a most serious—the most serious— violation of human rights. It should not be justified by any claim that it is necessary to safeguard other human rights. Surely the law cannot warrant any state's intervening by force against the political independence and territorial integrity of another on the ground that human rights are being violated, as indeed they are everywhere.

The claims that democracy justifies the use of military force by another state are no stronger. All the framers of the Charter purported to believe in democracy. They were hardly agreed as to what it meant, but they were agreed that force was not to be used against another state even to achieve democracy, however defined. Over forty years later states are still not agreed as to what democracy means, but they are still agreed that it is not to be achieved by force. The Charter would be meaningless if it were construed or rewritten to permit any state to use force to impose its own version of democracy. Such a view of the Charter would permit "aggression for democracy" against any one of

100–150 states by any self-styled democratic champion. That is not the law; it could not become the law; it should not be the law.

Nor is interstate force the solution to the scourge of terrorism, or even a significant deterrent to it. Little of contemporary terrorism is in fact perpetrated by states; too many states condone it, but surely the law does not—ought not—permit the use of military force against any state that does so. Even where a state is satisfied that another state has in fact perpetrated an act of terrorism against its diplomatic personnel, it is undesirable to permit the victim state to respond by military force against the territory of the perpetrator. The exceptions in article 51 were limited to cases of armed attack that are generally beyond doubt; a state's responsibility for acts of terrorism is rarely beyond doubt and difficult to prove to international satisfaction. Article 51 gives a right of self-defense, a right to use necessary and proportional force to defend against an armed attack. This right does not allow retaliation for past attacks. The response in self-defense to an armed attack must be necessary and proportional; an attack on the territory of a state perpetrating terrorism cannot be a "proportional" response and can hardly be the "necessary" response to defend against an act of terrorism already committed or even to deter future terrorist acts. The international community must develop stronger determination and seek other remedies against terrorism. A state that has been the victim of an act of terrorism will have to pursue other remedies against states that it believes responsible and against the states that encourage, promote, condone, or tolerate terrorism or provide a haven to terrorists.

The Charter—an epitaph to Hitler—is not neutral between democracy and totalitarianism, between justice and injustice, or between respect for human rights and their violation. Surely states are entitled—indeed, pledged and required—to promote democracy, justice between and within states, and respect for human rights. But the Charter and the international system have been and remain firm in their conclusion that those fundamental and ultimate goals are not to be pursued by force. With respect to the use of force, the Charter is neutral between democracy and totalitarianism. Neither may use force against the other. No state may use force to achieve either democracy or totalitarianism.

Intervention and Counterintervention

The difficult legal issues for the future continue to be those of military intervention and counterintervention. They are not resolved by the court's opinion in the *Nicaragua* case, and there is need—and room—to develop norms within the spirit and the letter of the Charter.

The attempt to regulate military intervention has suffered from asymmetries that are inherent when an international system, consisting of states represented by incumbent governments, is compelled to address internal change and from the difficulties of definition and drawing lines in complex, confused internal and international situations. The governing principles should not be controversial. The international system favors voluntary cooperation between states and between their governments. International law does not forbid one state to sell arms to another state, and upon authentic invitation, a state may introduce military forces into the territory of another to assist the government for various purposes, including maintaining internal order. On the other hand, a state may not introduce arms or armed forces into a country without the consent of its government, surely not to support any groups hostile to the government. In sum, a state may sell arms to an incumbent government, but not to any rebels; it may provide forces to help a government maintain order, but not to help any group disturb the order of an incumbent government.

That asymmetry, however, begins to erode as rebellion succeeds or moves to civil war. At some stage, the law's partiality to the incumbent government ceases, and it is no longer lawful for another state to help either the incumbent or its adversaries by military force (perhaps even by sale of arms). The Charter's fundamental commitment to state autonomy requires that states allow internal developments in another country to have their way. External forces must not significantly affect the territorial integrity of the receiving country or its political independence. Hence, external forces may not be introduced to help effect or prevent secession or to assist either side in civil war. The difficulty is that one cannot measure when aid to a government stops being that and becomes intervention in civil war.

That is the command of the law of the Charter. It has often been flouted. Inevitably, especially in an ideologically divided world, unlawful military intervention on one side has invited counterinterventions. Some commentators have supported the view that if a state has unlawfully intervened on one side of an internal struggle, another state should be permitted to counter that intervention. That view may come within the law of the Charter if the counterintervention is designed to "neutralize" the unlawful intervention and its effect on the political independence and territorial integrity of the troubled country. Above all, the right to counterintervene does not include the right to attack the third-state intervenor. (In Vietnam, criticism of American policy on grounds of international law did not flare up until U.S. forces attacked North Vietnam and Cambodia.)

Like the law of the Charter on the use of force generally, the law on intervention does not make ideological distinctions. As a matter of law, states are free to sell arms to, advise, and help incumbent governments to maintain order, whether they are more or less authoritarian, totalitarian, or democratic. A state may not intervene to help rebels, whether against a totalitarian or a democratic regime. If external forces intervene on one side of a civil war, perhaps other states may intervene on the other, but again regardless of the ideology of either side. It is as unlawful, for example, for the United States to give aid to the contras or to UNITA (in Angola), as it is for others to aid communist insurgents in the Philippines. In a civil war, it is not lawful to help either side, regardless of ideology. If one side is being helped by one state (in violation of law), an argument can be made that the law should permit counterintervention but not attack on the state intervening on the other side, again regardless of ideology.

The law of the Charter needs clarification and perhaps modest modification in regard to counterintervention. It largely permits remedies and responses not involving the use of force. But with respect to the terrible uses of force, it is important that, as far as possible, rules not be subject to concealment and distortion of facts and circumstances and to self-serving characterizations.[35]

Interventionary wars are not necessarily less terrible than those at which the Charter aimed. For such wars, however, the international system may require different norms and different kinds of commitments from major powers. The withdrawal of Soviet forces from Afghanistan, successful arms control agreements, and a determination to pursue further negotiations, as well as improved relations between the United States and the USSR generally, may contribute to a relaxation of the actions that have led to violations of the law of the Charter and to interventions and counterinterventions. That may make it possible for the United States to explore and negotiate as to what the law ought to be. It is not out of the question for the United States and the USSR to agree, in time perhaps formally, on a statement of understanding as to the state of the law and on their commitment to maintaining it by their own self-restraint, by restraining others, or by revitalizing the United Nations to that end.[36] Together the United States and the USSR also can press a few recalcitrant states to refrain from terrorism and to prevent the use of their territory as a base for terrorism.

More than forty years have not left the Charter unscathed, but neither have they proven that it is not viable or desirable. The world would not be better off without it. The world would not draft a better law. In 1989 there is some reason to hope that the big powers might yet agree to cooperate and to recommit themselves to the law of the Charter. Whether or not they agree, it is in the interest of the United States to reassume leadership for a world committed to that law, for a world of law and order.

NOTES

1. See George F. Kennan, *American Diplomacy, 1900–1950* (Chicago: University of Chicago Press, 1951), pp. 95–99.
2. I consider (and reject) the argument that the failure of the original conception and other "changed circumstances" have vitiated the law of the Charter, in *How Nations Behave,* 2d ed. (New York: Columbia University Press, 1979), pp. 137–39.
3. United Nations General Assembly Resolution 2625, October 24, 1970; and Resolution 3314, December 14, 1974.
4. An early report of the secretary-general spoke of "indirect aggression": where a state, "without itself committing hostile acts as a State, operates through third parties who are either foreigners or nationals seemingly acting on their own initiative." The concept has been construed to include "certain hostile acts or certain forms of complicity in hostilities in progress." United Nations Document A/2211, October 3, 1952.
5. See United Nations General Assembly Resolution 34/22, November 14, 1979; Resolution 35/6, October 22, 1980, and annual resolutions thereafter.
6. See United Nations General Assembly Resolution 38/7, November 2, 1983; and note 28 in this chapter.
7. One argument is that colonialism is a form of aggression and that states are justified in assisting the victim of aggression. See pages 44–45 in this chapter.
8. United Nations Security Council Official Records, 987th meeting, pp. 10–11, 988th meeting, pp. 7–8, December 18, 1961.
9. *International Legal Materials,* vol. 7 (1968), pp. 1323–25.
10. Third World states led the General Assembly to declare: "In their actions against, and resistance to, such forcible action in pursuit of the exercise of their right to self-determination, such peoples are entitled to seek and to receive support in accordance with the purposes and principles of the Charter." (United Nations General Assembly Resolution 2625, October 24, 1970.)
11. *International Legal Materials,* vol. 7 (1968), pp. 1323–25.
12. Final Act, Conference on Security and Cooperation in Europe. "Declaration on Principles Guiding Relations between Participating States" (Helsinki, 1975).
13. N. Michael Reisman, "Coercion and Self-Determination: Construing Charter Article 2(4)," *American Journal of International Law,* vol. 78 (1984), p. 642.
14. Oscar Schachter effectively demolished that suggestion in "The Legality of Pro-Democratic Invasion," *American Journal of International Law,* vol. 78 (1984), p. 645, responding to Reisman.
15. In addition to the suggested exceptions noted here, it has been argued that a state may intervene by force to help another state "modernize." Wolfgang Friedmann cited this proposal "only to illustrate the variety as well as the absurdity of the many criteria suggested to justify intervention" in

"Intervention and International Law," *International Spectator,* vol. 25 (1971), pp. 40 and 59–61.

16. Since article 51 is an exception to article 2(4), it was written to apply to member-states, which were bound by article 2(4). The prohibitions of article 2(4) subject to the exception of article 51 are now customary law applicable to all states. Compare article 2(6) of the Charter.

17. The failure of the Security Council has not been deemed to enlarge the exceptional right of self-defense under article 51. Compare p. 38 in this chapter.

18. Letter from Mr. Webster, secretary of state, to Lord Ashburton, British plen., August 6, 1842, *Webster's Works,* VI, 301–302, in John B. Moore, *Digest of International Law,* vol. 2 (1906), p. 412.

19. The United States asserted instead the right to act pursuant to authorization from the Organization of American States.

20. Statement of April 14, 1986, in *Department of State Selected Documents,* no. 20 (Washington, D.C., 1986). The United States did not bring Libya before the Security Council, as self-defense under article 51 contemplates and probably requires.

21. See United Nations General Assembly Resolution 41/38, November 20, 1986. A resolution of condemnation in the Security Council (5/18016/Rev. 1, April 21, 1986) received nine votes, but was not adopted because the United States, the United Kingdom, and France vetoed it. Some U.S. writers justified the bombing. See Gregory Francis Intoccia, "American Bombing of Libya," *Case Western Reserve Journal of International Law,* vol. 19 (1987), pp. 177, 187–89. See generally Christopher Greenwood, "International Law and the United States' Air Operation Against Libya," *West Virginia Law Review,* vol. 89 (1987), p. 933.

22. The court concluded that it could not decide the case under the Charter because of a reservation by the United States, and would therefore decide it only under customary international law. But the Court held that customary law and the law of the Charter were essentially congruent in relevant respects, in effect construing the Charter.

23. Case concerning *Military and Paramilitary Activities in and against Nicaragua (Nicaragua v. United States of America),* Merits, 1986 ICJ REP. 14.

24. The judgment was by a 12–3 vote on most of the key issues. Two of the judges in the minority dissented not from the court's substantive conclusions, but from its decision to reach the substantive issues; they therefore did not address those issues.

25. During the early postwar decades, the international system took strong positions in support of the law of the Charter. It rejected the Arab states' claim that they were justified in using force to prevent the creation of the State of Israel. It strongly supported actions to meet the North Korean aggression against South Korea. It rejected claims of the Soviet Union that the Charter had no relevance for convulsions within the communist world such as the communist coups in Czechoslovakia in 1948 and Hungary in 1956, effected with the aid of Soviet troops. It rejected expanded notions of permissible force in self-defense, as by the United Kingdom and France against Suez (1956).

26. A brief bloody confrontation—the Soccer War—took place between Honduras and El Salvador in 1969.

27. In a notable instance, the United States characterized the war in Vietnam as an attack by an independent North against an independent South. It thus created a case of armed attack in which it could help South Vietnam in collective self-defense and could even attack the territory of the aggressor. Others saw Vietnam as a civil war between North and South, with the United States intervening on one side, or as a civil war in the South with competing interventions by North Vietnam and the United States; from that perspective they questioned U.S. intervention and, particularly, its bombing of North Vietnam, Laos, and Cambodia.

    Various justifications by (or on behalf of) the United States action in Grenada also were widely disbelieved or rejected. See p. 54 in this chapter.

28. U.S. policy as regards uses of force by other states has also appeared recently to be less committed to the Charter. Notably, in the Iran-Iraq War, though it would seem that Iraq had initiated hostilities in violation of article 2(4), the United States in effect "proclaimed neutrality" and even began to "tilt" against Iran. At the beginning of that war, U.S. attitudes were doubtless shaped by the resentment of the recent Iranian hostage crisis.

    The impression that the United States was less firmly committed to the law of the Charter was supported by evidence that the United States has moved generally to "unilateralism" rather than cooperation, particularly the kind of cooperation reflected in the rule of law; for example, the decision to bring down a friendly (Egyptian) plane in an attempt to capture a suspected terrorist; the refusal to appear in the *Nicaragua* case; termination by the United States, after forty years, of its declaration accepting the compulsory jurisdiction of the International Court; abandoning the Law of the Sea Convention after fifteen years of negotiation; and continued refusal to adhere to international human rights treaties. Limited resort to the International Court of Justice (as in the *Gulf of Maine* case) and the prospect of imminent U.S. ratification of the Genocide Convention were applauded but were not sufficient to offset the general impression of "unilateralism."

29. The Reagan administration did not claim any single legal justification for the invasion of Grenada, and champions of the action also provided diverse justifications, based on particular assumptions and characterizations of the facts. See the articles in the *American Journal of International Law*, vol. 78 (1984), pp. 131–75, and a communication from the legal adviser of the State Department appears in the same issue on pages 661–65. In fact, few observers in or outside the United States accepted those asserted facts and characterizations as the authentic reasons for the invasion, and it appears not unwarranted to treat Grenada as an instance of Reagan "doctrine" or "policy" that asserts the right to use force to impose or restore democracy where communism threatens.

30. The United States did not admit to covert actions by the United States at the Bay of Pigs (1961) or in Chile (1973) and therefore did not justify them as legal. In the Dominican Republic (1965), the United States declared that organized government had broken down and U.S. troops were needed to

preserve order so as to protect lives, but some have seen that action as a precursor of the "Reagan policy."

31. The administration will have to face other questions implicating international law, such as whether to accept the jurisdiction of the International Court of Justice and whether to adhere to human rights treaties.

32. Apologists for some U.S. actions were prominently quoted as saying that if what the United States wished to do is prohibited by international law, "too bad" for international law. See, for example, the editorial "Lawyers Invade Grenada," *The Wall Street Journal,* November 1, 1983, p. 30; and Michael A. Ledeen, "When Security Pre-empts the Rule of Law," *The New York Times,* April 16, 1984, p. A21.

33. This would include the USSR. Like other countries sometimes charged with violating the Charter, the USSR has never pleaded guilty. But in asserting its innocence, it has not purported to reject the law of the Charter or even to reconstrue it; rather, it gives its own version of relevant facts. Thus, in Hungary, Czechoslovakia, and Afghanistan it claimed that its forces entered by authentic invitation of the authentic government to assist that government in maintaining order, and Soviet forces were therefore not engaged in any use of force against the territorial state. Only in the Brezhnev Doctrine did the USSR in effect admit to deviating from the Charter, and that "exception" has probably been abandoned. See pp. 43–44 in this chapter. The USSR would no doubt support the mass of states in resisting any change in the law of the Charter.

34. Also, the United States has justified its attack on Libya in response to terrorism, but it condemns Israel for similar responses to terrorism.

35. That is why the Charter prescribed, and the International Court of Justice confirmed, the requirement of an armed attack to make force permissible. That is why armed attack should not be lightly construed to cover incidents—even terrible terrorist incidents—limited in scope and usually committed in ways that make it difficult to determine who is responsible. That is why permissible responses must be strictly limited in geography and in scope to what is proportional and necessary to defend (not to retaliate, even in the hope of deterring).

36. As suggested in Soviet President Mikhail Gorbachev's statement to the United Nations on December 7, 1988. Excerpts of Gorbachev's speech can be found in *The New York Times,* December 8, 1988, p. A16.

3

ETHICS AND RULES OF THE GAME BETWEEN THE SUPERPOWERS

Stanley Hoffmann

The use of force by the United States and the Soviet Union in the conduct of their respective foreign policies raises ethical issues that transcend and, in many respects, eclipse international law. The ethical framework within which the superpowers act and react significantly influences the unwritten rules of the game that often dictate whether a superpower will resort to military force or seek out avenues of cooperation. In recent years the rules of the superpower game have been influenced, and some would argue changed, by the emergence of the so-called Reagan Doctrine. This provocative stratagem for the use of military force (spearheaded with American support) to roll back Soviet expansionism and reciprocate for the evil designs of the Brezhnev Doctrine strikes at the core of the contest between the superpowers. International law may help to discern the novelty of the Reagan Doctrine, but an inquiry into the ethical aspects of the rules of the game between the superpowers will reveal even more about where the Reagan Doctrine is leading American foreign policy and whether that direction is the preferable one.

The relevance of ethics to the use of force preceded the rise of the superpowers to the dawn of history. The questions one asks today also were those of past generations. What kinds of ethical norms are, and should be, proclaimed and practiced by the actors on the world stage? How do rival conceptions of the "good" clash and sometimes compromise in an anarchic milieu, and what happens when one of them prevails? How much leeway for moral restraints and imperatives is there in that peculiar branch of politics we call international relations? What could be called the ethical system of international relations includes the moral beliefs of the actors, but it also includes legal norms, international regimes, and regular practices that have not been formally codified in treaties and do not have the solemn characteristics of customs.

Because the other contributors to this book focus on international law and its application to the use of force, I will examine first the ethical foundations of international law. These stand in stark contrast to the uncodified ethical bases of political systems, both past and present, which I discuss throughout this chapter. My objective is to identify rules of the game between the superpowers, including those rules that are existential in character and those that are deliberate ones. The ethical dimensions of these rules will tell us much about the superpower contest and how the use of force can serve or impair the ends of peace and justice. Understanding this ethical system also will help us to understand the moral issues that confront the Reagan Doctrine and the alternative ways in which the superpowers can continue their global contest without becoming addicted to the use of force.

ETHICAL FOUNDATIONS OF INTERNATIONAL LAW

The relation of ethics to law is complex. Much of international law is technical. But that part of it concerning the political relations of states, the use of force, and states' main economic activities deserves to be studied in connection with ethics. If one examines both why legal rules are adopted and why they are obeyed, one finds three categories of foundations.

The first foundation is coercion, such as the coercion found in peace treaties imposed by the winners on the losers. Nothing about this is necessarily ethical, unless the war that has been won was a "just war," and the terms of settlement were equitable. On the other hand, to rule out coercion as inherently immoral would doom a very large fraction of international law.

The second foundation is reciprocity. Whether norms established and enforced on such grounds are ethical or not depends on the nature of the deal and the subject matter of the norm. But even if the deal is highly technical or remote from ethical considerations, the idea of reciprocity itself has a moral component, which is the recognition of a mutuality of interests and of the need to base international order on the idea that many such interests deserve mutual respect.

The third foundation is a belief in the common good. This means that one subscribes to a given norm, even if it is likely that observing it will not always be in any short-term or narrowly defined (in other words, selfish) interest and even if it may happen that other actors will not observe it, because one believes that this norm is right or that it is essential for the common welfare and happiness of international society. It is here that the connection with ethics is most direct and obvious. The law of the United Nations Charter and the various international conventions that deal with the use of force embody moral codes that not every commentator or actor embraces.

International legal norms bind the superpowers as well as other states. But, as I have argued elsewhere,[1] the special solemnity of law is something great powers are often suspicious of. It impedes their freedom of maneuver insofar as it sets up serious constraints. Violations entail high costs precisely because of the visibility and thickness a legal barrier entails. As a result, superpowers often prefer informal arrangements to solemn agreements. A consideration of superpower ethics must include both their relationship to international law and the nature of such informal arrangements. I will say little about the former, which is discussed elsewhere in this book, particularly by Louis Henkin, with whose analysis I agree. I will concentrate here on the informal arrangements.

ETHICS OF POLITICAL SYSTEMS IN HISTORY

Every political system in the past, like all other institutions, can be submitted to moral judgment along the lines I have tried to suggest in *Duties beyond Borders,* or according to the quite similar

73

criteria—ends, means, and consequences—Joseph Nye has indicated in his writings.[2] In order to be able to apply moral judgment to an institution, one does not have to assume that moral concerns figure prominently in the calculations of those persons who have set up the institution or who make it function. What makes moral judgment possible is quite simply that every institution has a moral dimension. Whatever the motives of its leaders or of its members—motives that are often very difficult to ascertain not only for outside observers but for the subjects themselves—it is necessary to distinguish what could be called the inherent morality of the institution from the explicit, or deliberate, morality or immorality of the policies pursued by its leaders. This is precisely where a consideration of the means and procedures used by the institution and a consideration of the effects it has on its members and on outsiders are essential.

Ever since the end of the dream of a Christian world community—in other words, ever since the appearance of the modern territorial states—international relations have constituted what Hedley Bull has termed an "anarchical society."[3] It is anarchical because of the absence of any common superior and also because of the vagueness or poverty of common norms. But anarchy in international affairs is not synonymous with chaos. Competition can take dampened and regulated forms. Different processes of cooperation are always going on, at least among some of the members of the international system. It is a bounded anarchy, insofar as the system has its own institutions, which Bull, among others, has described, for the maintenance of a modicum of order. How much of the society the international system actually constitutes is a matter of empirical investigation.

One could argue that concrete international systems have oscillated between two extreme ideal-typical poles. At one end is the ideal type of balance-of-power systems. They can be found, so to speak, at the moderate end of the realist spectrum, if one considers that realism—the view of international affairs held by such diverse writers as Thucydides, Hobbes, Hans Morgenthau, Raymond Aron, and Kenneth Waltz—remains the dominant paradigm in the study of international affairs. Balance-of-power systems correspond to the view that order in international affairs is the first priority and comes, for instance, before any concern for justice. Moreover, the establishment and maintenance of order require the great powers to curtail their ambitions. This curtailment is assured by the various techniques of the balance of power, which range from different modes of cooperation among the major powers to wars aimed at preventing a troublemaker from destroying the existing equilibrium.

Balance-of-power systems have the virtues of flexibility and moderation, but they subordinate to the requirements of order—narrowly defined as the equilibrium among the major actors—such important ethical values as peace and justice. While one goal of the balancing of power is to prevent the kind of general war that could mean the destruction of the system, more limited types of war are freely resorted to as instruments of order. This is possible as long as the objectives of such wars are kept limited and as long as the technology of warfare does not make limitations impossible.

As for justice, the problem posed by order arises especially, although not exclusively, in the relations between the major powers and the lesser ones. The latter are, at best, submitted to severe constraints by the great powers, which may respect the formal independence of the small states, but often restrict their external freedom of action and interfere in their domestic affairs. At worst the independence of a smaller state can be sacrificed to the ambitions and calculations of the great powers, as in the case of the partitions of Poland. Moreover, balance-of-power systems have left ample room for the constitution of vast empires in which justice was certainly not the main consideration.

At the other extreme one finds the various kinds of revolutionary systems, including the bipolar competitive ones, such as the Greek city-state system dominated by Athens and Sparta. Here, either incompatible and unrestrained state ambitions or rival ethical-political systems clash. What prevails is what Raymond Aron called an ethics of strife,[4] a division of the world into friend and foe, accompanied by losses on all the ethical dimensions—those of peace, justice, and order.

ETHICS IN THE PRESENT INTERNATIONAL SYSTEM

If we turn to the present international system we are confronted both with ambiguity and with originality. On the one hand, the opposite principles embodied by the United States and the Soviet Union illustrate an unending sharp ideological struggle. Each superpower represents a principle of international order and legitimacy, as well as a principle of domestic political and social organization opposed to the principles of the other side and incapable of full worldwide success short of the elimination of the rival.

On the other hand, the operations of the postwar international system actually resemble closely those of balance-of-power systems. As in the latter, a considerable degree of flexibility and moderation has been evident. Flexibility exists in the sense that the system has survived enormous changes in the distribution of power since 1945. For instance, the colonial empires broke up, and many new nations appeared; communist China defected from the Soviet alliance system. Moderation has prevailed in the relationship of the major powers, the most notable example being relations between the United States and the Soviet Union. Far more even than in balance-of-power systems, vast areas of institutionalized cooperation have emerged in the form of global or regional international regimes. Thus the evidence suggests some order despite the division of the world into two camps, despite the growing inequality between the rich and poor, and despite the domestic fragility, multiplicity, and heterogeneity of so many of the units that, cobbled together, reveal the murky contours of order.

What ethical judgment can be passed on the present "anarchical society"? Today's international system can be seen as ethically unsatisfactory from two very different viewpoints. The more extreme one condemns it as inherently evil and practically equivalent to a state of war. According to this view, the system should be seen not as an international order at all but as a vicious struggle between incompatible conceptions for the establishment of order. The existence of nuclear weapons makes this struggle particularly repugnant, given not only the danger their possible use represents but also the importance of nuclear threats in the basic policies and strategies of the main contenders. From a second, more moderate perspective, the present international arrangements undoubtedly are flawed, but many of those flaws, insofar as they result from the heterogeneity—or, rather, the multiple heterogeneities—of the system and from the ideological battle between Washington and Moscow, are unavoidable.

For two reasons I categorically reject the view that the present system is inherently evil. Empirically, this view does not account accurately for the way in which states actually behave. Neither superpower has confused hostility with war. Raymond Aron made this point many years ago; likewise, John L. Gaddis has more recently observed that the theory of deterrence as it has been formulated in the United States implicitly accepts the point made by George Kennan in his influential writings of 1946–1947 about the difference between hostility and war.[5] Moreover, accepting the first perspective would have ethically intolerable consequences in the present international system, a point to which I will return later. I find myself therefore much more in agreement with the view that the present international arrangements are undoubtedly, but also unavoidably, flawed. I am not, however, as resigned to their imperfections as that view could easily lead one to be.

— In analyzing the ethical aspects of the present scheme of world order, I will apply the framework I tried to set up in *Duties beyond Borders,* one based on liberal values. It is concerned with peace, a value whose importance has been enhanced by nuclear weapons. It is concerned with order, both in the somewhat negative form of the preservation of an equilibrium of power that requires superpower restraint and in the form of various cooperative arrangements, particularly where the absence of cooperation would lead to chaos because of the inability of actors in an interdependent world to solve common problems unilaterally or conflictingly. It is concerned with justice, especially in the forms of human rights and distributive equity. It is, of course, aware of the frequent tensions between these values in the real world, but it does not sacrifice any of them to the others. It shows some faith in the possibility of reasonable accommodation.

THE NATURE OF THE RULES OF THE GAME

That the superpowers have established some rules, often by trial and error, in order to regulate their competition cannot be denied. Do these rules constitute a "regime"? An international regime entails not a transfer but a pooling of sovereignty, a commitment to or a practice of joint rather than unilateral action. It results in the gradual transformation of the way in which the national interest is calculated: a less contentious, narrow, or selfish definition of the short-term interest, as well as a greater consideration of the long-term interest, even if it conflicts with the short-term one. Regimes consist of norms and procedures that provide the participants both with restraints and with opportunities. They therefore constitute a formula for order (insofar as they assure a modicum of predictability and methods for the settlement of disputes), as well as for peace (insofar as the avoidance of violence in the settlement of conflicts is essential). They do not necessarily constitute a formula for justice, which depends on the very substance of the norms and on the nature and effects of the procedures.

The present superpowers' "game" does not constitute an overall regime. The norms and procedures tend to be implicit, not explicit, except in some very specific instances. According to Robert Keohane, regimes entail "cooperative, diffuse reciprocity."[6] In the relations between the superpowers, we often find no cooperation at all, but a tit-for-tat exchange of hostile acts. When cooperation exists it is, at best, specific rather than diffuse, and often very fragile. Overall, the superpowers demonstrate no preference of joint action over unilateral action. Undoubtedly partial regimes exist, especially in the nuclear realm. This has been ably argued by Michael Mandelbaum in his work on the "nuclear regime" and by Joseph Nye, who has examined the arms control agreements between the superpowers and the nuclear nonproliferation regime.[7] The superpowers' overall relationship constitutes even less of a regime than the security practices of past balance-of-power systems.

What then do the rules of the superpower game constitute? My analysis relies on the writings of Hedley Bull and John Gaddis, as well as on some of my previous essays.[8] I would suggest a fundamental distinction not between legal norms and informal rules of behavior, but between "existential" and "deliberate" rules. The existential rules derive from the very nature of the superpowers' "condition." The deliberate rules are those the superpowers devised in order to carry out the existential ones.

Existential Rules of the Game

The superpower game has two kinds of existential rules. The first kind is the rules of nuclear deterrence, which is, as McGeorge Bundy has reminded us, a condition more than a policy.[9] It is a condition created by the nuclear revolution. This revolution, for reasons that need not be stated once more here, has enormously boosted the reasons for prudence in the behavior of states (what Joseph Nye has called the crystal ball effect,[10] or what game theorists refer to as the shadow of the future), although prudence is not guaranteed to prevail forever.

The nuclear revolution also has changed the way in which the balancing of power takes place. In the present international system, by contrast with the operations of past multipolar systems, the central nuclear strategic balance is not a matter of state coalitions. However, in contrast to past bipolar systems, the balance of terror in the nuclear age has been remarkably robust because of the deliberate rules of stability devised by statesmen and strategists, and because of technology, which has made defense ever more difficult. Thus, a dangerous spiral of defensive and offensive measures and countermeasures has been checked. Technology also has made possible the "reconnaissance revolution," which has allowed the superpowers to get around the deadlock over inspection.

The second set of existential rules relates to the superpowers' competition, another condition characteristic of any anarchic international system, and of the modern one in particular. Among these rules, one can list the impossibility for either side to "renounce ideology." While economic, military, and even political détente is conceivable, ideological muting (not to mention disarmament) is very difficult to imagine. One can also list the implicit recognition of the right of each side to use its instruments of power abroad, including the search for allies and clients. Finally, the implausibility of a superpower condominium is an existential rule dictated by both East-West reasons (essentially the American unwillingness to regulate the world in partnership with the repugnant Soviet regime) and North-South reasons (the resistance of third countries to any superpower dictation).

Deliberate Rules of the Game

Deliberate rules of the superpower game can be found in the nuclear realm and in the political one. It is important to understand that "deliberate" is not synonymous with "explicit." Many of the rules discussed below have not been explicitly formulated in written agreements, but have been devised and followed nevertheless.

In the nuclear realm three kinds of rules must be mentioned. The first set aims at preserving the central balance. Each superpower not only has competed with the other, but has deliberately taken measures to avoid falling behind the other (a situation very different, say, from the competition between France and Britain on the one hand and Germany on the other in the 1930s). Both sides have viewed falling behind as a destabilizing condition that, under certain circumstances, could incite either the "winner" or the "loser" to preempt. The formula for a stable balance that each superpower has developed over the years means having an invulnerable retaliatory force whose effect is to discourage an enemy first strike, having a vulnerable population that discourages oneself from striking first, and building up nuclear counterforce capabilities and conventional forces in order to make nuclear deterrence more plausible.

The second category of rules in the nuclear realm aims at reinforcing stability either through unilateral measures, such as the permissive action links employed in nuclear weapons systems, or through explicit agreements. Here we find the various measures of arms control agreed upon by the superpowers, such as the Anti-Ballistic Missile Treaty of 1972, the various limits on offensive weapons in the SALT I and II agreements, the superpowers' hot lines, the regulation of incidents at sea, and the nuclear nonproliferation regime, which constitutes the only element of limited condominium. This is one area in which the superpowers' relationship has been codified and international law plays its usual role.

The third and most important set of rules in the nuclear realm has been the taboo on the actual use of nuclear weapons, even though occasional explicit threats have been made—on the Soviet side usually for bluff, and on the American side for very limited purposes. In other words, nuclear arms have been treated as very special weapons.

In the political realm also, three sets of rules can be listed. First is the imperative of avoiding direct military confrontations between the superpowers, if necessary by deliberate measures of self-denial. (The United States, while helping the Afghan resistance in the 1980s, carefully avoided any direct intervention in the war in Afghanistan. The Soviet Union acquiesced in the mining of Haiphong and the bombing of Hanoi in 1972 and in the bombing of Tripoli in the spring of 1986.) The avoidance of direct military confrontations sometimes has taken the form of ad hoc policies, and sometimes that of actual agreements to neutralize such areas as Antarctica, Austria, and the seabed. It has entailed a recognition of the inviolability of the status quo in Europe. Until now, at least, each superpower has refrained from military attacks on a major ally of the rival. The United States did not attack China when it was allied to Moscow, nor has it attacked Cuba. The Soviet Union never has attacked either Western Europe or Israel.

The second set of political rules pertains to crisis management. These rules have had two aims: to find a negotiable way out of direct confrontations, as in various Berlin crises and during the Cuban missile crisis, and to prevent third parties from entangling one of the superpowers in a confrontation with the other. Sometimes this has been achieved because one of the superpowers, or even both, stayed out of dangerous affairs. For example, the Soviet Union did not back China against the United States at the time of the Chinese-American confrontation over Quemoy and Matsu. Both Washington and Moscow refrained from intervening in the India-Pakistan War of 1971 and in the Iran-Iraq War of the 1980s. Sometimes one superpower has avoided a confrontation with the other over a third party by limiting the wreckage and restraining its own client. This has been the case repeatedly in the Middle East.

Third, each of the superpowers has recognized the "legitimate interests" of the other. This has meant, on the one hand, the recognition of spheres of influence (Central America for the United States, Eastern Europe for the Soviet Union), including the careful avoidance of direct military intervention in those spheres and abstention from attempts at provoking defections there. (This goes beyond the formal recognition of the inviolability of borders through force that is part of the 1975 Helsinki agreements.) On the other hand, the superpowers also have tried to maintain essential "rules of civility" between the limits set by their competition. The way in which civility and competition can be combined was demonstrated in the Daniloff case of 1986.

Such is the substance of the deliberate rules. As for the way in which they have been established, three main factors seem to have been decisive. One has been the learning experience between the superpowers themselves. Each has tried to derive lessons from earlier failures or earlier events in order to pursue its interests in ways that do not jeopardize peace but preserve a certain amount of order. Another, especially on the American side, has been the pressures of allies whose interest in safeguarding both balance and peace has been constant. (After the collapse of détente in the late 1970s, the Soviet Union's Eastern European allies played a comparable role.) Finally, frequent pressures by third parties have been aimed at curtailing the more devastating effects of the superpowers' competition.

ETHICAL IMPLICATIONS
OF THE RULES OF THE GAME

What are the ethical implications of these existential and deliberate rules, in particular from the perspective of the core liberal values discussed above? Both a positive and a negative dimension are discernible.

On the positive side, one finds reintroduced into the potential jungle that is the present international system some elements of order and predictability, which both bipolarity and nuclear weapons—and, above all, the combination of the two—make absolutely essential. Nothing is more positive than the preservation of what could be called central peace: the avoidance of war between the superpowers. This can be compared, in modern history, only with the European situation that existed between 1815 and the outbreak of the Crimean War (a period of thirty-eight years, compared with the more than forty years of the nuclear era). From the liberal viewpoint, the fact that in the major part of the world the competition of value systems continues—in other words, the fact that pluralism has prevailed—is also undoubtedly a major asset.

On the negative side, however, many features deserve to be judged critically. In the first place, some of the rules of the game have evil aspects. The recent debate about the ethics of deterrence has concentrated on the evil of threatening to inflict massive damage on one's rival and has illustrated that the very credibility of deterrence depends on the willingness to carry out such a threat. Defenders of deterrence have replied that it is often necessary to run a small risk (the risk that deterrence will fail) for very large stakes. The real question is that of the long-term psychological and political consequences of nuclear deterrence, none of which is more disturbing than the constant search for new weapons systems and the evidence of the failure of deterrent postures to constrain the force structure on either side.

The morality of spheres of influence also is open to question. A sphere of influence is an area within which one side's power is allowed to prevail unbalanced. This often provides a license for brutality, with the result that the order being maintained is both violent and unjust. The moral critique of spheres of influence could be extended to a questioning of the whole sphere of economic interdependence, which is that of the world capitalist economy. It is a domain in which the United States is the dominant power. While the problem of violence does not arise here, what does arise is the issue of justice, just as it was raised by Great Britain's domination of the world economy in the nineteenth century.

Second, several of the rules of the game are quite fuzzy. For example, the scope of spheres of influence is uncertain. Soviet probes in Berlin, the Soviet encouragement to or tolerance of the North Korean invasion of South Korea, the Soviet deployment of offensive missiles in Cuba, and the ambiguity about Afghanistan in 1978–1979 show that neither side is entirely clear about what constitutes a vital sphere to the other. Therefore, attempts to change the limits of an inviolable sphere cannot be avoided.

The substance of what constitutes influence also is unclear. One need not go back to the fundamental disagreement between the Western powers and the Soviet Union about what actually was conceded to Moscow in Eastern Europe by the Yalta agreements; the Helsinki agreements also contain obscurities. The Soviet Union's clear recognition of the sphere of American predominance in Central America does not seem to prevent Moscow from sending arms to its allies in the area. In other words, even the rather primitive and debatable form of order that spheres of influence ensure is not guaranteed. Nor are the rules about the central balance necessarily very clear. We are all too familiar with the clash of theories about what kinds of forces deter best.

Third, we must realize how sharply limited are the current rules of the game. In the world of superpowers they are less extensive than the rules that once existed among the major actors in balance-of-power systems. This is particularly the case insofar as the relations between the big players and the smaller ones are concerned. In the present international system, dangerous threats to peace, order, or justice could, and often do, come from the small powers. The "disciplining" capabilities of the superpowers are very limited because the kind of great power condominium that can play a deterrent or even a punishing role in this connection is lacking, and the risk-free unilateral intervention by one of the superpowers is not always certain. Greater opportunities therefore exist for small powers to strut on the stage and wreak violence, especially if the lesser actor has been intelligent enough to receive an assurance of support from one of the major rivals. (Examples are Nasser, Qaddafi, or Assad in the case of the Soviet Union, and the shah of Iran in the case of the United States.) Also, even though an incipient condominium exists in this domain, the ability of the superpowers to prevent the proliferation of nuclear weapons has not been unlimited. Thus, whereas in balance-of-power systems great powers often assured order at the expense of justice, now they often provide neither.

Fourth, the network of rules contains serious gaps. No rules of positive cooperation exist that would assure a regular flow of assistance to the Third World, a vast and complex area in which the relationship between the superpowers remains primarily competitive. Nor do the superpowers' "rules of civility" encompass a sufficiently large zone of activities. At least until recent Soviet statements, which remain rather abstract, the attitudes of the superpowers about terrorism were sufficiently different to prevent an extension of those rules to this particularly troublesome area.

Fifth, the rules of the game have a Sisyphean aspect. They are inherently contradictory, since they constitute an attempted compromise between, on the one hand, the old principle of sovereignty and competition exacerbated by bipolarity and by the ideological nature of this particular rivalry, and, on the other hand, the attempt at restraining the worst effects of the contest.

In the nuclear realm the contradiction has taken two forms. One is the self-undermining of deterrence through the arms competition. A paradox is at work here. The very effort to preserve the central strategic balance has led to disturbing effects because of the evolution of technology. The development of multiple warheads and of precise and smaller nuclear weapons has undermined the treatment of nuclear arms as different from other arms. The new technologies have created what I have described elsewhere as three dangerous new possibilities.[11] The apocalyptic possibility is the temptation each side may have in a major crisis to strike first at the vulnerable systems (weapons, satellites, command and control) of the other. The race to defensive systems in space risks having the same effects. The second peril is the temptation either side may have to resort to a limited use of nuclear weapons in the hope of being able to prevent escalation and to limit damage, a hope that might turn out illusory. The third danger is that of a return to conventional wars even between the superpowers because of an excessive confidence in their ability to prevent nuclear escalation. The ill-begotten conventional war all too easily could lead to a nuclear one, especially in areas of great importance to these powers.

The same fundamental contradiction accounts for the grave deficiencies of arms control. A tendency can be seen for every weapon that has not been regulated through arms control to become either a bargaining chip or immune from arms control because of its intrinsic strategic value. The result is an indecisive race between stability and destabilization insofar as crisis stability, arms race stability, and political stability are concerned. Here too, technology has played a disruptive role, with new weapons developments, such as mobile ballistic missiles and cruise missiles, creating new obstacles to verification. Thus, in the nuclear realm the contradiction between sovereignty and restraints threatens order and ultimately peace, especially if one takes into account the effects of some of the developments on third powers that may be tempted to provide for their own security rather than rely on the guarantees of a superpower.

In the political realm the second form of contradiction has resulted in the decentralization of violence. Incapable of achieving gains through force in the more important areas, the superpowers have engaged in an often frantic quest for marginal advantages, thus frequently provoking the very crises that need to be carefully managed. This exercise is indeed Sisyphean in essence. It also reminds one of an old Chaplin short movie: Poor Charlie, in order to make some money as a remover of snow, offered his services from house to house. He piled snow removed from the front yard of each house into the front yard of the next house, whose bell he then rang! The decentralization of violence takes the form of constant superpower interventions in and manipulations of the domestic affairs of smaller powers.

The uncertain balance between continuing competition and crisis management led, in the late 1970s, to the doom of détente. The failure of détente was caused by different notions of reciprocity, the Soviet conception being quite specific and the American one rather diffuse. It also was caused by different expectations. The United States wanted to deter Soviet expansionism through carrots and sticks; the Soviet Union aimed at weakening American containment and at moving toward a condominium. Turning the limited agreements of 1972 and 1973 into a ratification of the status quo thus proved impossible.

The complications in the political and nuclear realms come together in one unresolved issue: the geographic location of nuclear weapons. The deal that resulted from the Cuban missile crisis in 1962—the removal of Soviet missiles from Cuba and of American ones from Turkey—was merely a way of getting out of a particularly dangerous crisis. But it could not serve as the basis of a general rule, given the geopolitical differences between the two sides. As a result, new and serious tensions arose when the United States introduced intermediate nuclear forces into Europe in 1983.

THE LEGITIMACY OF THE RULES OF THE GAME

An examination of the ethical aspects of the superpower rules of the game inevitably raises the problem of the legitimacy of those rules. One might say that an institution, or a system, is legitimate if its good aspects prevail over the bad ones. The current paradox lies in the difference between those aspects of the super-power rules that concern the relations between the rivals and those pertaining to their relations with third powers. The relations between the superpowers involve a mix of the good and the bad, but so far at least the good is seen as more important.

On the plus side we find the avoidance of major superpower crises since 1962 and the resumption of arms control negotiations. On the minus side, we find a certain shrinking of the common code in the past few years. One potential problem is the risk that either of the superpowers, or perhaps both, may become so dissatisfied with the restraints that the rules impose on their influence abroad that a peaceful and orderly resolution of the next crisis may become impossible.

As far as the relations between the superpowers and third powers are concerned, the bad aspects predominate. We have witnessed many attempts by smaller powers to exploit the super-powers' contest for their own particular and local interest (for example, in the Middle East, Syria, and Israel). We also have witnessed many proclamations by third powers of the illegitimacy of the superpower rules. The nations of the Third World have condemned superpower attempts to force them to recognize the existing international hierarchy, as, for instance, in the Treaty on the Non-proliferation of Nuclear Weapons. This amounts to a rejection by the smaller states of the most traditional formula of order that prevailed in past international systems. Often, the smaller states have condemned the violence of the superpowers. They have condemned the superpowers' indifference to Third World economic demands and thus denied that the superpower rules constituted an acceptable basis either for order or for justice. The spread of state and nonstate terrorism is in part a consequence of this illegitimacy.

THE REAGAN DOCTRINE

In what directions should the superpowers go? Two strategies are at present engaged in a somewhat muted, confused, but important contest.

One is the direction recommended by the proponents of the Reagan Doctrine. On the surface it has a certain attractiveness. What is the Reagan Doctrine—which at its core is the offer of military and logistical support to anti-Soviet forces in areas currently dominated by clients of Moscow—if not the deliberate pursuit of such Western values as individual freedom and democracy in areas where these values are suppressed, where such a pursuit is not dangerously explosive, and where armed conflict can be waged at reasonably low cost?

Moreover, the Reagan Doctrine means no more than a return to symmetry. In the past, the Soviet Union supported anti-American or anti-Western forces in the Third World without ever experiencing the sting of Western support for anti-Soviet elements in areas under the control of Moscow or Moscow's allies. In other words, the Reagan Doctrine could become the basis for a new rule of reciprocity, imposing a new norm of restraint on Soviet behavior comparable to the restraints observed by the United States in areas under Soviet influence.

However, it is hard to accept the direction set by the Reagan Doctrine as politically or ethically justified. Politically, what this new attempted norm suggests is that the Soviet Union refrain from intervening not only in the traditional American sphere of influence but indeed in the whole world, with the notable exceptions of the Soviet Union itself, its East European glacis, and perhaps Cuba and Vietnam. In other words the whole world, minus the Soviet sphere, would become the American sphere of influence. The Soviet Union is most unlikely ever to accept such a norm. Also, for a policy to become the basis of a norm of behavior, it needs sufficient domestic support, at least in the case of a norm developed in the United States. It is not at all clear that such a basis exists. Finally, whether the political results of the pursuit of the Reagan Doctrine are minimal or maximal, whether they amount to a mere prolongation of civil wars or to the actual overthrow of governments, the Reagan Doctrine would make the forces of competition in the international system win a round over the restraints.

The Reagan Doctrine is even more objectionable on ethical grounds than it is on legal grounds, which are ably discussed elsewhere in this book. The costs may be low for the United States, but we in fact would impose extremely heavy costs on the innocent populations that would be the victims of the subversive or insurrectionary movements we supported. Indeed, the costs may be far heavier for those populations than for the regimes we are trying to weaken or to destroy. Moreover, the moral worth of the forces we supported is, to put it mildly, highly uneven. Finally, Robert W. Tucker makes a decisive argument: for the policy to be effective and to impose genuine losses and a change of behavior of the Soviet Union, we would have to take exceedingly dangerous risks.[12]

To conclude, it is not at all clear that the pursuit of the Reagan Doctrine would serve the cause of human rights and justice. As for the other important values—order and peace—it is precisely their importance that has explained, in the past, why the "cold warriors" themselves chose a policy of containment rather than one of roll-back or liberation. The Reagan Doctrine is nothing but a new, warmed-over version of the old roll-back doctrine. Its likely effects are neither order nor peace nor democracy.

STRENGTHENING NORMS
AND SUPERPOWER COOPERATION

Liberal internationalists and in recent years academics more than politicians have suggested the second direction the superpowers might take. In this view, order requires both the strengthening of norms against military aggression (hence the justification of aid to the resistance in Afghanistan, a clear-cut case of invasion) and a strengthening of the elements of cooperation between the superpowers.

Peace requires the enhancing of crisis stability, both by unilateral moves concerning, in particular, the composition of one's nuclear forces and through negotiation so that time would be available to the superpowers should a serious crisis break out.

This strategy heightens the importance of successful arms control negotiations aimed, above all, at removing destabilizing and unverifiable weapons systems. Peace also requires far greater attention to the problem of decentralized violence. This means major efforts for regional settlements in Central America and in the Middle East and for the establishment of at least partial security regimes in such areas with the participation of the superpowers. Justice requires a gradual loosening of the hold of the superpowers on their respective spheres, which in turn presupposes a lessening of the intensity of their competition. Justice also requires that each superpower pay far more attention to the demands and needs of other powers.

These are familiar points. While the direction is clear and attractive, at least to liberals, the road obviously is an exceedingly rocky one. For suitable rules of the game to develop along such lines would require extraordinary changes in Soviet external behavior. Such changes are happening under present circumstances, given the pressure of domestic economic problems, the rather negative balance of costs and benefits produced by the quest for influence abroad, and Soviet President Mikhail Gorbachev's cooperative approach to international relations. For these changes to last and to expand, extraordinary changes also would be required in the Soviet domestic regime and in the national sense of insecurity that existed long before the Soviet regime itself. In dispelling this sense, the United States has a major role to play, by responding imaginatively to the innovations Gorbachev has introduced.

Indeed, the responsibility of the United States should not be underestimated. As one of the two nuclear superpowers and as the world's most powerful economic actor, the United States clearly plays a major role in the establishment of ethically legitimate rules of the game. The United States cannot play such a role whenever it allows domestic priorities to prevail in its economic policies and thus tries to force others to pay the costs of its own mistakes or mismanagement.

Nor can the United States play the role it should play when it allows domestic fantasies about America's decline or about the

Soviet threat to dictate its foreign policy, as it did in the late 1970s. The United States cannot play a useful role when the fragmentation, discontinuities, and contradictions of its constitutional system make any coherent diplomacy difficult, or when past frustrations divert it from the indispensable quest for effective international institutions not only in economic or monetary affairs but also in the realm of security. These are areas in which conflictive moves tend to boomerang and unilateral ones bring few of the expected rewards.

For the United States to move in the direction of strengthening norms and cooperation with the Soviet Union, particularly for the purpose of controlling the use of force, it will have to redefine its conception of security, to change its priorities in order to pay greater attention to the problems of justice, to focus more on the long term, and to put bargaining ahead of unilateral action in a world that finds itself "after hegemony."[13]

NOTES

1. Stanley Hoffmann, "International Law and the Control of Force," in Karl Deutsch and Stanley Hoffmann, eds., *The Relevance of International Law* (New York: Doubleday, Anchor Books, 1971), pp. 34–66.
2. Stanley Hoffmann, *Duties beyond Borders* (Syracuse: Syracuse University Press, 1981); and Joseph S. Nye, Jr., *Nuclear Ethics* (New York: Free Press, 1986).
3. Hedley Bull, *The Anarchical Society* (New York: Columbia University Press, 1977).
4. Raymond Aron, *Peace and War* (New York: Doubleday, 1966), part 4.
5. For the most recent restatement, see Raymond Aron, *Les dernières années du siècle* (Paris: Commentaire Julliard, 1984); and John L. Gaddis, "The Long Peace," *International Security*, vol. 10, no. 4 (Spring 1986), p. 119.
6. Robert Keohane, "Reciprocity in International Relations," *International Organization*, vol. 40, no. 1 (Winter 1986), pp. 1–27.
7. Michael Mandelbaum, "Nuclear Weapons and World Politics," in David C. Gompert et al., eds., *Nuclear Weapons and World Politics* (New York: McGraw-Hill, 1977), pp. 15–74; and Joseph S. Nye, Jr., "Nuclear Learning," *International Organization*, vol. 41, no. 3 (Summer 1987), pp. 371–402.
8. See Bull, *The Anarchical Society;* and Gaddis, "The Long Peace." See also Stanley Hoffmann, *Janus and Minerva* (Boulder: Westview Press, 1986), chs. 5 and 6.
9. McGeorge Bundy, "The Bishops and the Bomb," *New York Review of Books*, June 16, 1986.

10. Nye, *Nuclear Ethics*, p. 61.
11. Hoffmann, *Janus and Minerva*, ch. 5.
12. Robert W. Tucker, *Intervention and the Reagan Doctrine* (New York: Carnegie Council on Ethics and International Affairs, 1985).
13. Robert Keohane, *After Hegemony* (Princeton: Princeton University Press, 1984).

4

THE PRINCIPLES OF FORCE, THE FORCE OF PRINCIPLES

William D. Rogers

The focus in this inquiry of the Council on Foreign Relations has been nothing if not ambitious. We have attempted to say something basic about the way nations behave toward each other and whether a system of constraints that is fairly called law inclines them to use force in their own self-defense and in the collective defense of their friends.

The question is a pervasive one in contemporary international relations. It is at the heart of the relationship of the two superpowers. It affects all of the regional conflicts in the developing world—in Central America, the Horn of Africa, Mozambique, Angola, Afghanistan, and Southeast Asia. In each, outsiders have inserted their aid, weapons, or troops into an internal conflict over national power. Whether a law exists that regulates force bears vitally on the vast diversion of resources to military purposes throughout the world. The norms of articles 2(4) and 51 of the United Nations Charter are the central geopolitical issue of our time—whether limits on the threat or use of force constitute a basic organizing principle of relations between states in the modern world.

Ours has been a fact-driven inquiry. This is typical of all inquiries into the question of the role of force. There is no doubt about preferences. The sentiment is universal—it was certainly so among those who participated in the study group, and it informs the writings included in this publication—that given a choice, all would prefer to see a world so organized. Political violence is by definition destructive of human values.

But the ideal is rarely reality in the affairs of nations. As the authors in this volume make clear, and as the common experience of mankind demonstrates, the ideals of the Charter have not been fully realized in our world.

The Charter was intended to alter the essential nature of the international community. It was drafted in the closing days of the worst, most devastating war the world had ever experienced. Its overarching purpose was to ensure that history not repeat itself. The 1945 effort was one of soaring ambition—the culmination of the work of decades—to impose a rule of law on the use of force. The idealistic campaign to propagate international arbitration in the late nineteenth and early twentieth centuries, inspired by Andrew Carnegie, the Kellogg-Briand Pact, and the League of Nations, foreshadowed the Charter's flat proscription on the nondefensive use of force. The ultimate design of the UN scheme was to make war both impossible and illegal—impossible, through a concert of the great powers functioning as the Security Council; illegal, by condemning all use of force except that justified by the necessities of self-defense. This commitment to self-restraint was enacted in a solemn multilateral treaty, sanctified by all of the panoply of ritual and legitimacy that the traditions of international law could muster, and embraced ultimately by virtually all of the 160 nations of the world community. It was at bottom a fundamentally conservative instrument.

Many saw the Charter as a proclamation of a new era in the history of mankind, one in which every member of the community of nations renounced the use of force in the conduct of its relations with all others. Law was perceived as an instrument for the achievement of mankind's highest aspiration: the permanent peace of nations.

As subsequent events show, the ideals set in 1945 were not to be that easily realized. The world has not rid itself of the threat of war or the use of force by one nation against another. Expenditures for the tools of war by the nations of the world continue apace. Even in constant dollars, the cost of armaments today compares unfavorably with that of the years of World War II.[1] And the instruments of violence have become increasingly devastating in the forty-four years since the Charter. Nuclear weapons are a surfeit. Either superpower can destroy the militarily significant targets in the other many times over. France and Britain also possess the capacity for massive intercontinental nuclear damage. The threat of a nuclear Armageddon is increasingly ubiquitous. Nuclear arms are spreading to Pakistan, Brazil, Israel, and South Africa. The ability to conduct violence with sophisticated weapons, once monopolized by the industrialized nations, is now found throughout the world. Developing countries maintain vast armies. North and South Korea between them have a million and a half men under arms.[2] A number of Third World countries can compound poison gas. Biological weapons of hideous potential are within the grasp of virtually every nation, if not every terrorist.

War has been a common feature of the postwar landscape. States have regularly sent their forces across international borders or supported indigenous attacks on national authority in other countries. Thus, in the past decade alone, Argentina invaded the Falkland Islands, Nicaragua supported the insurgents in El Salvador, Libya invaded Chad. The United States bombed Libya, South Africa invaded Angola, and Mozambique attacked Uganda. Ethiopia has waged regular war in the Horn of Africa. The Polisario challenge to the regime of Morocco has received outside assistance. The Iran-Iraq conflict raged for almost a decade. China attacked Vietnam and India. Vietnam invaded and occupied Cambodia, while China offered support to the Khmer Rouge guerrillas. The Soviet Union invaded Afghanistan. The United States overwhelmed Grenada.

Two aspects of the contemporary situation, however, distinguish our own age from experience before the Charter. The first is that no war has been fought among any of the industrialized powers: Europe, North America, and Japan have been at peace with each other since 1945. The second is that the United States and the Soviet Union, the two nations capable of conducting another world war, have held back. Though each superpower has often deployed its armed forces with palpably coercive intent and has used those forces in combat on a number of occasions since 1945, neither has done so against the other or against a professed ally of the other. The United States has fought against the communist states of North Korea and Vietnam, instigated the 1961 invasion of Cuba, and provided weapons and logistic support to anticommunist insurgencies in Afghanistan, Angola, Nicaragua, and Cambodia. The Soviet Union has used its own troops in Czechoslovakia, Hungary, and Afghanistan, and has aided the forces of violence elsewhere. But it has not since 1945 attacked or supported an attack on a democracy. Nor has the United States been a party to the use of force against any member of the Warsaw Pact.

In short, the Charter has not achieved eradication of war as a "scourge of mankind." But World War III has not occurred. This has been a supreme achievement of the community of nations. The past forty-four years has been a reign of peace among the world powers, standing in remarkable contrast to the awesome devastation of the wars of the industrial powers that punctuated the years from the middle of the nineteenth century to the middle of the twentieth.

Is this evidence of the force of law in the world?

The Charter is the crown jewel of the legal constraints on the use of force. But no one in the study group seriously argued that the mere existence of the Charter text proved the existence of an effective regime of law. By the same token, no member of the study group suggested that since 1945 states have complied consistently with the Charter's regime. Indeed, tested against the standards of articles 2(4) and 51, most participants found historical violations by both superpowers, by many (but not all) of the other industrial nations, and by a number of Third World nations.

In truth, all states are torn by opposing considerations; the greater the power, the greater the dilemma. All have an interest in defending their boundaries against external intrusion and in conserving such share of the current distribution of privilege and wealth as they may enjoy. All, in short, have in differing degrees some vested interest in the status quo and thus in reinforcing the international legal system that helps maintain the complex relationship among states. Nations also have a contrary interest in being able to take advantage of such power as they may have, of translating what is only potential into actual benefit. Thus, the possession of force is not without consequence. Force is seen to have its uses. To possess it is an incentive to employ it. In those instances in which power can be decisive in relationships between states, limitations on the use of power constrain a comparative advantage of the more powerful.

But power is not what it used to be. In relative terms, those nations that have historically been weaker have vastly enhanced their ability to shoot back. In absolute terms, the destructive capacity that the United States, the Soviet Union, and the other major powers can deploy is orders of magnitude greater than before. But with modern weaponry, the weak can now inflict severe damage on a stronger opponent. Nicaragua, nicely managed by a corporal's guard of U.S. Marines in the first third of the twentieth century, now has such firepower as to compel any would-be invader to deploy several divisions.

New constraints on the exploitation of that power—moral considerations, the likelihood of costs and penalties imposed by other states, damage to investment and financial interests abroad—have reduced the temptation to resort to force. States are increasingly disinclined to use the force they have at hand. The destructive power nations could deploy is in growing disproportion to the force they actually use. Nations are increasingly aware of these new realities and are inclined to act in their own self-interest in ways that are consistent with the principles of international law.

Perhaps, then, we are witnessing a change in the trend lines of violence. Several regional conflicts—including those in Afghanistan, Angola, and Cambodia—are evidently on the way to resolution. It is not inconceivable that historians will look back on the last third of this century and conclude that the incidence of violent conflict between nations declined. In the main, the stability of international boundaries has been greater since the Charter's promulgation then it was in the first four decades of the twentieth century. Aggression in the classical form and wars motivated by pure territorial conquest are relics of the past. They are not entirely out of fashion, as Colonel Qaddafi demonstrated when Libyan forces invaded Chad. Indeed, conventional wars between national units fighting across international boundaries have characterized the history of the Middle East for four decades, both in the recurring conflicts of the Arab-Israeli confrontation and in the eight-year Iran-Iraq War. But perhaps even these cycles of violence have exhausted themselves. Elsewhere in the world, the predominating forms of war in the post–World War II era have been waged within state borders, often pitting local governments against local insurgents.

As further circumstantial evidence of the force of the Charter law, Louis Henkin points out that accused states using force universally justify their actions in legal terms as legitimate self-defense. States do not behave as though there were no law. The debates in the United Nations between state leaders, and in less authoritative circles among academics, over whether the latest military event is justified revolve not around the norms but around the facts. The principles that make the aggressive use of force illegitimate are usually assumed; the International Court of Justice suggests that this fact confirms the existence of a common understanding that the use of force has been and should be governed by law.

A considerable body of hardheaded commentary in the postwar period has claimed that law and national interest are at odds with each other and that the latter must at the end of the day win out. In point of fact, the two are not so inconsistent. The very notion that law should narrowly limit the use of force to legitimate instances of self-defense represents a vital contribution to the national interest of every member of the world community of states. Leaders know it. In this sense, the nurturing of respect for the principles of nonuse of force ought to and indeed does affect the actual behavior of states.

But if the deliberations of the study group showed anything, and if one point is perfectly plain in the thinking of those who contributed to this volume, it is that the Charter's principles are maddeningly imprecise on the edges. And at the edges—in cases that do not fit the classical characteristics of a national armed invasion—is where the controversies rage. Charter principles, particularly article 2(4), are an open invitation to debate.

Imprecision breeds uncertainty. Uncertainty breeds evasion. And article 2(4) is abstraction piled on abstraction. Who can define a "threat" to use force in a way that will give clear guidance for all purposes and in all future crises? Who can define "political independence"? Who can say, indeed, what "force" is? If it were possible to define universal constraints on the use of force with precision, nations would surely behave differently. Indeterminacy has an identifiable effect on what states do. It is not cost-free.

Some have suggested in response that the norms are very like a constitution in their generality. All constitutions require explication in the framework of specific cases. The process of explication over time can build up an edifice of understanding as to the true meaning of the text.

But experience does not give much encouragement to this hope in the case of the Charter norms. The almost half-century since the Charter was signed has not made the world much wiser about the real meaning of self-defense or its precise application. We are more puzzled now than ever about the contours of the principle. The hard cases have not really made any law. We now know from the Israeli attack on the Iraqi nuclear facility in 1981 that preemption presents analysts with a conundrum. As the Nicaraguan conflict has revealed, it is difficult to define precisely what is or ought to be a permissible response to cross-border subversion or arms supplies to insurgents in a third country. Grenada illustrated the slippery nature of collective regional legitimation of the use of force. And what of admitted strategic weapons' targeting of civilian population centers, or the unwillingness of the superpowers to renounce the first use of nuclear weaponry? Are these not implicit threats? Indeed, what is deterrence if not a credible threat to use force? And is not deterrence the very essence of the remarkable stability of the post–World War II system?

The contributions to this volume amply demonstrate the difficulties in the application of the article 2(4) norm. Those who opened this volume expecting simple and definitive answers to all questions relating to the legal constraints on the use of force are undoubtedly disappointed.

Furthermore, the central premise of article 2(4) is that states should stay out of each other's way. Thus, strictly interpreted, the Charter rule inhibits—to the impatience of Jeane J. Kirkpatrick and Allan Gerson—the right of one nation to support those seeking to change the way another nation is governed. Sovereign separateness is the essence of the Charter's rule; each nation must keep its hands off every other nation when it comes to the "use or threat of force." But does not a principle so firmly based on sovereign separateness swim against the tide of current world affairs? National autonomy is eroding. We are increasingly interdependent, as we are regularly reminded. Interdependence, if it means anything, means the porousness of nation-state boundaries and an increased vulnerability to external circumstance and considerations. Human rights are no longer exclusively domestic issues; trade, finance, and investment are more and more the subject of multilateral regulation, having burst the bonds of strictly national concern; what happens to the tropical rain forests and the oceans affects us all. The consequences of a state's action are not limited to the boundaries of that state.

Thus, in the relations of nations, not to act is to act. The more interdependence, the more difficult it is to distinguish the legitimate from the illegitimate effects of one nation on another. As Talleyrand said, "Nonintervention [is] a metaphysical and political word which signifies about the same thing as intervention."[3]

The Charter principle has become the abstract standard against which uses of force have been notionally measured. It certainly cannot be said that the statesmen of the world have ignored article 2(4). Indeed, one is struck by how ubiquitous its formula has become. The fact that it can be pressed into service in justification of such a wide variety of actions has made it a kind of portmanteau, capable of expansion or contraction to suit the volume and shape of the contents to be carried. Thus, the United States, in embracing the Panama Canal treaties, promised that, in exercising its rights to keep the canal open, it would avoid the use of force against the political independence and territorial integrity of the nation of Panama.[4] In the recent Angola–Namibia–South Africa accords, the parties, which had been at each other's throats for over a decade at considerable cost in blood and treasure, vowed to eschew the use of force against each other in the future.[5] The utility of the soaring aspirations of article 2(4) was most vividly illustrated recently by none other than the secretary-general of the communist party of the Soviet Union, Mikhail Gorbachev, in his December 7, 1988, address to the United Nations, when he said:

> It is obvious . . . that the use or threat of force no longer can or must be an instrument of foreign policy. This applies above all to nuclear arms, but that is not the only thing that matters. All of us, and primarily the stronger of us, must exercise self-restraint and totally rule out any outward-oriented use of force.[6]

Nothing if not the threat of "outward-oriented use of force" has allowed the Soviet Union to maintain its hegemonic grip on the nations of Eastern Europe. Its own "outward-oriented use of force" battered back the national rebellions in Hungary and Czechoslovakia. Yet Gorbachev was speaking in what has become a great tradition. The Charter lies easily in the mouths even of leaders of nations who threaten and on occasion resort to force. That Gorbachev could invoke the idiom of article 2(4) at a moment of triumph in international politics says something about its practical utility as a guide to state behavior.

It is quite possible, as Louis Henkin so ably demonstrates, to construct an internally consistent elucidation of the core principles of the Charter with but a measure of ambiguity at the fringes, one that provides reasonable guidance in the bulk of cases to those leaders who may be inclined to ask whether particular uses of force are legal or illegal. The central difficulty, however, is that states facing crises that touch on their national interest and security have not been inclined to ask whether a contemplated use of force is legal and pay much attention to the answers.

The Charter norm, however, is by no means the only principle of international relations speaking to the appropriate use of force. In fact, a spectrum of constraints exists. They range from the abstract and the general to the concrete and the highly specific. Stanley Hoffmann illuminates the rich fabric of principles restraining the use of force by the superpowers against each other. Articles 2(4) and 51 may be taken as one end of that spectrum.

Richard Nixon and Leonid Brezhnev tried to set down some slightly more explicit rules governing conflict avoidance by the superpowers in the 1973 basic principles agreement.[7] The agreement did not attempt to address the issue through restraints on the use of force, but rather through a description of the kind of responsible political behavior which would reduce the risk of forceful confrontation—commitments to renounce special privilege, to eschew "unilateral advantages," and to coexist peacefully. The agreement recognized a special need for restraint in the dealings of the United States and the Soviet Union with each other. Action, whether involving the use of force or not, that threatened the continued existence of either or represented an effort by one to steal a march on the other, by altering the balance between them unilaterally, threatened stability and therefore was prohibited.

These principles were more concrete than the Charter. Although they were explicitly limited to the U.S.–Soviet relationship, they were still quite general. They proved incapable of imposing real restraint on national behavior. The Soviets quickly accused the United States of a breach by conniving with Anwar Sadat to arrange their expulsion from Egypt. Washington persuaded itself that the Soviet Union had scrapped the agreement when it engineered the Cuban intervention in the Angolan War in 1975.

Other efforts have been made to define the general guidelines by which the Soviet Union and the United States—and thus the world—might avoid the ultimate conflict. A number of groups, of which the American Committee on East-West Accord has in some ways been the most far-reaching, have focused on regional conflict as the most volatile tinderbox capable of igniting a superpower war. The committee has argued for a prohibition on the direct or indirect use of combat forces or covert activity by either the Soviet Union or the United States in any Third World insurgencies. This would represent a general rule applied to each of the regions of present conflict.

A further variant, more adaptable and realistic, is a specific ad hoc understanding between the two powers on acceptable intervention behavior in particular regions or countries. Such understandings can represent a marked advance beyond the generality of article 2(4). They avoid an attempt to draw a general rule to govern all cases around the world. A commitment to restraint in one conflict does not require a party to say how it will behave everywhere. This may be more practical. It reflects the way nations behave. The actual conduct of foreign relations, whatever the persistent demands of those out of office for a disciplining strategy, is more fact-specific than principle-oriented.

But the strength of such a practice can also be its weakness. By providing that force may not be used in one area, it may imply a tolerance for the use of force in others. If such an agreement implicitly condones an intervention, it can become the legal basis for the acceptance of a sphere of influence.

Of these ad hoc understandings, the one that emerged from the Cuban missile crisis has been perhaps the most impressive for its long record of peacekeeping accomplishment. In essence, John Kennedy and Nikita Khrushchev agreed that the Soviet Union would remove its missiles from Cuba in exchange for a U.S. commitment not to invade the island so long as no offensive weapons were there. The principle proved useful in defusing both the 1970 crisis over the establishment of a base in Cuba to service Soviet submarines and the controversy stirred up in 1979 by the appearance in Cuba of Soviet MIG-23 fighter-bombers.

The superpowers have not reached many other such successful specific accords for defusing potential conflict in regional crises. Perhaps a parallel example is emerging in the Namibia–Angola–South Africa accords, which enjoy the active support of the Soviet Union, as well as the United States. The Afghanistan agreements may represent another. Such arrangements, fact-specific and limited in time and space, may be the most promising of techniques for creating a body of law restraining the use of force in the modern world.

In addition to specific regional understandings are the several agreements of positive law governing a wide variety of matters relating to the accumulation and deployment of the instruments of force: specific limitations on the quantities of weapons or their location or the transparency of information about them. These are often embodied in treaties and other written instruments of law.

States also occasionally declare their intention to abide by self-restraining ordinances. These can be statements of intent, gentlemen's agreements, or unilateral statements noted by the other side that are expected to evoke some cooperative response. And, finally, there are the implicit rules of the game.

The web of undertakings that can restrain the use of force in international affairs, in other words, is complex, going far beyond the simple words of the Charter. In the struggle toward a rule of law for the community of nations, the choice is not between the Charter norms and chaos. The choice is between the Charter and other means to fill in the corners of an incomplete canvas. These may be less ambitious. But they may also be more realistic. It probably makes little difference whether scholars classify these principles as law. The response of one state to a perceived breach of a solemnized undertaking by another does not turn on a technical definition of whether treaty language has been violated or even whether the arrangement is "law" as such or "binding." Nor is it decisive that the perceived restraint is incorporated in an exchange of promises ratified in treaty form pursuant to domestic jurisprudence. If a principle restrains the aggressive use of force or turns aside a threat to do so, it is irrelevant whether that principle is contained in a treaty, a gentlemen's agreement, an implicit representation that certain consequences will follow, or the grand injunctions of the Charter.

The restraints on the use of force that find expression in these various measures cover a considerable range of determinacy. They extend from the fuzzy abstractions of the Charter and similar efforts, such as the Kellogg-Briand Pact, to the mathematical precision of territorial delimitations on weapons deployment and bean-counting rules in arms control agreements. Taken in the main, though, a fair examination of the historic record would suggest a correlation between determinacy of a particular principle and its observation. The central question may be not whether a restraint is law but whether it is precise. Perhaps the more precise it is, the more a principle behaves in the way law is supposed to behave by having a consequential impact on the way nations act.

The Charter, in short, is an ideal. It is universally embraced as an aspiration. The real work of providing a law to restrain the use of force, however, may well be the more modest but more precise instruments of specific agreement. The experience of the era since the Charter suggests that these can make up in utility what they lack in universality.

NOTES

1. Stockholm International Peace Research Institute, *World Armament & Disarmament Yearbook* (Stockholm, 1986).
2. Institute for Strategic Studies, *World Military Expenditures* (London, 1987–1988).
3. Foreign and Commonwealth Office, "Is Intervention Ever Justified?" *Foreign Policy Document,* no. 168 (London, 1984), p. 33.
4. Panama Canal Treaty, September 7, 1977, article 5, TIAS 10031.
5. Agreement among the People's Republic of Angola, the Republic of Cuba, and the Republic of South Africa, December 22, 1988. Reprinted in *Department of State Selected Documents,* no. 32 (Washington, D.C., 1988).
6. Address to United Nations General Assembly, December 7, 1988. Transcribed in *The New York Times,* December 8, 1988, p. A16.
7. Basic Principles of Relations Between the Soviet Union and the United States, reprinted in *Department of State Bulletin,* vol. 66 (Washington, D.C.: United States Government Printing Office, June 26, 1972), p. 898.

5

USE OF FORCE AFTER THE COLD WAR: PANAMA, IRAQ, AND THE NEW WORLD ORDER

David J. Scheffer

The end of the Cold War was a seminal legal, as well as political, event in world history. The two major protagonists of that forty-five-year struggle—the United States and the Soviet Union—began to retreat from the controversial interpretations of international law that they had employed to justify the use of force and that had left such deep imprints on the decade of the 1980s. The Soviet government turned inward to cope with its rebellious republics, while the United States unilaterally launched a controversial invasion of Panama and then groped its way toward a "new world order" by liberating Kuwait with a devastating assault on the Iraqi army authorized by the United Nations Security Council.

In July 1989 Soviet President Mikhail Gorbachev implicitly repudiated the Brezhnev Doctrine,[1] which Jeane J. Kirkpatrick and Allan Gerson describe in chapter 1 as the Soviet Union's rationale for enforcing a "principle of socialist self-determination" upon the Soviet bloc.[2] Throughout 1989 and 1990 the Soviet military occupation of Eastern Europe collapsed as one nation after another broke loose from the Soviet empire and developed its own pluralistic form of government. The Soviet Union ceased to be an interventionist superpower, although the central government repeatedly affirmed its willingness to use force to discipline its constituent republics.[3] The reconstituted Supreme Soviet began to assert its own legal authority to participate in use-of-force decisions as Soviet military policy veered toward isolationism.[4]

The Reagan Doctrine, which had so centrally defined American foreign policy in the 1980s, revealed its transitory character when the end of the Cold War deflated the ideological contest between the United States and the Soviet Union. As Soviet military support for repressive regimes declined, the legal premise for lending reciprocal military support to insurgencies fighting such regimes necessarily suffered. With the arrival of democracy in Nicaragua in early 1990, the Reagan Doctrine lost its primary target and, in turn, its audience. Some of the other regional conflicts of the Reagan era—in Cambodia, Afghanistan, and Angola—survived into the 1990s. But the American role in these conflicts increasingly shifted from one of substantial, indirect military intervention (promoted with the ideological fervor that characterized the 1980s) to one of seeking accommodation with the embattled governments and cooperating with the Soviet government to search for peaceful settlements in each case.[5]

A new generation of bilateral and multilateral agreements on arms control and on postcommunist Europe lessened the prospects of a nuclear exchange between the superpowers and of a third world war erupting on the European continent.[6] At the United Nations, the rhetoric of the new era was being translated into cooperative ventures among the permanent members of the Security Council and other major powers.[7] The euphoria that seized West and East Germans when the Berlin Wall was breached on November 9, 1989, signaled the immense possibilities for peaceful change in the new Europe. Though the fast-paced political evolution of Europe would not be entirely free of violence, that which occurred was of a distinctly internal nature. The violent popular uprising in Romania in December 1989, which quickly led to the downfall of Nicolae Ceausescu's repressive government, succeeded in large part because the Soviet Union chose not to interject its troops to protect the embattled dictator. In fact, conventional wisdom was turned upside down when France and the United States indicated their willingness to endorse any Soviet military intervention that would defend the *populists*.[8]

Despite the revolutionary developments that unfolded in Europe during the final days of the Cold War, political evolution elsewhere in the world would not so readily embrace the legal principle of nonuse of force to achieve political aims. Two examples dominated the initial years of the post–Cold War era. The first was the American invasion of Panama in December 1989, which resulted in the apprehension of Panama's longtime leader, General Manuel Noriega, to stand trial in Florida on drug trafficking charges and in the installation of the previously elected government of Guillermo Endara. The second example was the Iraqi invasion and occupation of Kuwait in August 1990 and multilateral enforcement actions, authorized by the UN Security Council, that ultimately brought the defeat of the Iraqi army and the liberation of Kuwait. When examined together, the U.S. invasion of Panama and the U.S.–led multilateral response to Iraq's aggression do not form a consistent vision of the "new world order" President George Bush propounded during the Gulf conflict. Instead, they reveal the difficult choices that governments must make between the national interest, narrowly conceived, and the emerging global interest of the post–Cold War era. Much remains to be done before the principles and enforcement mechanisms of international law effectively constrain the aggressive use of military force. An equally challenging task will be the international regulation of both unilateral and collective uses of force for novel purposes—such as the protection of human rights within sovereign borders—that are not yet enshrined in international law.

PANAMA

Since the turn of the century, the United States has had a special relationship with Panama. President Theodore Roosevelt saw to it that the nation of Panama was carved out of Colombia for the express purpose of overseeing the construction of the Panama Canal.[9] American troops have remained stationed in Panama, notably in the area adjacent to the canal, throughout the nation's existence. The Panama Canal Treaty of 1977 renegotiated the arrangements formalizing the U.S. military presence in Panama. The treaty provides for the removal of all U.S. troops by the year 2000 and for Panamanian authorities' complete assumption of the administration and operation of the canal by that date.[10] The Neutrality Treaty of 1977 leaves permanently standing an American military guarantee to defend the neutrality of the canal.[11] At the time, it appeared that a peaceful dismantlement of U.S. rights to the canal (including the right to station thousands of U.S. troops there) would proceed unencumbered by political discord between the two nations.

Relations between the United States and the authoritarian government of General Noriega, however, steadily deteriorated during the 1980s. The antidemocratic character of Noriega's regime, as well as his alleged participation in the trafficking of narcotics to the United States, proved politically unacceptable to the Reagan and Bush administrations. In 1988 the Reagan administration imposed tough economic sanctions on Panama,[12] which precipitated the collapse of Panama's lucrative banking industry and devastated an economy dependent upon U.S. trade. As a candidate for president in 1988, Vice President George Bush successfully opposed concluding negotiations for a deal under which Noriega would step down from power if the United States dropped a federal indictment charging him with international drug trafficking.[13] The short-term political advantage had the effect of digging Bush deeper into the Panama dilemma once he assumed the presidency.

The American invasion of Panama in late 1989—and what it portends for international law and the use of force—must be understood in the broader context of two earlier phases of U.S.–Panamanian relations during the first year of the Bush administration.

Suffering under stiff economic sanctions, pressured by months of American-led negotiations to ease him from power, and personally targeted by a federal indictment for drug trafficking, Noriega conceded to hold national elections in May 1989. He then engineered massive fraud to rig the electoral count in favor of his hand-picked candidate, even though the opposition leaders reportedly held a three-to-one advantage.[14] Noriega thugs savagely beat the two top candidates, Endara and Guillermo Ford, before television cameras.[15] Bush had pledged repeatedly that Noriega must go and the elections were to have sealed Noriega's fate.[16] But Bush's choices, under international law, were limited.

Bush immediately dispatched 1,900 U.S. troops to Panama "to protect the lives of American citizens" and to augment the 10,300 U.S. troops already stationed there under the terms of the Panama Canal treaties.[17] He resisted pressures in Washington and from populists in Panama to use force against the Noriega regime to install Endara as the leader of a democratic government[18] and pressures to abrogate the Panama Canal treaties.[19] Bush's national security adviser, Brent Scowcroft, stated that the additional troops were being sent "to protect American lives and, if necessary, to protect the Panama Canal." He declined to characterize the deployment as one designed to restore democracy.[20] Rather than entertain calls to abrogate the Panama Canal treaties, Bush affirmed that the United States was "committed to the integrity of the Panama Canal treaties" and would "assert and enforce its treaty rights in Panama."[21]

As Louis Henkin points out in chapter 2, no principle of international law permits the use of military force to ensure the success of internal democratic processes.[22] Even Kirkpatrick & Gerson would have to agree that the Reagan Doctrine, strictly defined, did not purport to grant a license for military intervention to promote democracy where the ruling government is *not* receiving arms from the Soviet Union, the Soviet bloc, or other foreign sources. Both the Panama Canal Treaty and the Neutrality Treaty were ratified with amendments, conditions, reservations, and congressional testimony that clarify the limited circumstances under which the United States may militarily intervene in Panama. The Senate was exceptionally clear in establishing its intent to shield domestic Panamanian political events from military interference and to uphold the neutrality and operation of the canal as the basis for the right to intervene.[23]

113

Bush's restraint during the initial Panamanian crisis of 1989 reflected a keen appreciation for the maddening dilemma international law sometimes thrusts upon world leaders. A dictator's clear assault upon the rule of law at home will not necessarily translate into an attack on the rule of international law justifying another nation's military intervention. This was especially true in Panama, where the United States, only a decade earlier, had ratified treaties prohibiting such intervention.

Nonetheless, during the ensuing months two policy initiatives established the basis for an ultimate showdown with Noriega. The first was Bush's public encouragement of a coup or revolution to overthrow the Panamanian leader.[24] Although Bush counted primarily on Panamanians, particularly officers of the Panamanian Defense Forces (PDF), to overthrow Noriega, such official encouragement necessarily implied tangible U.S. support for an indigenous revolt. The second initiative was the futile mediation effort of the Organization of American States (OAS) to persuade Noriega to step down or, at a minimum, share power until free elections could take place. The Bush administration wanted the OAS to dispose of Noriega, while the OAS as a whole viewed its mandate as one of restoring democracy and self-determination, even if that meant allowing Noriega to retain some power for a limited time. Latin American governments also were inclined toward absolutist opinions about principles of sovereignty and nonintervention, and hence never embraced Washington's aggressive tactics toward the Noriega regime.[25]

The second crisis in Panama occurred on October 3, 1989, when within a span of hours Noriega quashed a military insurrection led by Major Moises Giroldi. The U.S. Southern Command (SOUTHCOM) chose not to intervene in a definitive manner to assist Giroldi's renegade troops, and thus helped seal their fate. But American conduct during and after the aborted coup raised disturbing legal questions and set the stage for the large-scale invasion of Panama on December 19.

On the morning of October 3, SOUTHCOM deployed forces on two "bottleneck" roads in Panama City, but refrained from directly intervening to support the Giroldi coup. Early official explanations stated that the troop deployments were limited to safeguarding American lives and rights of access under the Panama Canal treaties.[26] On October 6, Defense Secretary Dick Cheney disclosed that, contrary to other explanations, only one of the two deployments had been scheduled previously.[27] Officials confirmed that the two deployments responded to Giroldi's specific request for such assistance and that U.S. troops would have blocked pro-Noriega forces if the latter had made any attempt to reach PDF headquarters on either of the two routes.[28]

SOUTHCOM thus appeared to be implicitly collaborating with Giroldi to block certain key access routes under the pretext of exercising legitimate treaty rights. When, during the coup's most critical hours on October 3, Bush administration officials refused to authorize action beyond that initial blocking movement because of their professed doubts about Giroldi's credibility and whether this longtime crony of Noriega's was setting up the United States,[29] the "fog of battle" quickly descended upon government explanations and U.S. policy. Administration officials denied any American involvement in the coup attempt and thus any interference in Panama's internal affairs.[30] But the facts spoke otherwise.

Following the embarrassing events of October 3, the Bush administration began to distance itself from the public policy of nonintervention that it had followed after the May elections. The decision not to intervene with full force in the coup attempt begat a new policy of intervention.[31]

Three critical questions emerged. First, under what conditions should the United States directly intervene with military force to support an anti-Noriega coup in Panama? Secretary of State James Baker set the tone when he said that in Panama, the United States does not rule out the use of "either force that we ourselves plan totally and direct or force in conjunction with some other operation."[32] According to Bush administration officials at the time, the U.S. criteria consisted of the following:

- U.S. intervention must be strictly on a U.S. timetable, so that it is launched at a time of maximum opportunity and advantage.

- U.S. intervention must proceed in accordance with U.S. operational plans, not those of the coup leaders.

- U.S. authorities must have adequate information about the coup.

- The leaders of the coup must be well organized, explicitly request U.S. assistance, be clearly prodemocratic and preferably in touch with the political opposition, and be prepared to hand Noriega over to American authorities.

- The United States will await a good opportunity "to take advantage of an aggressive American spirit."[33]

Baker and other officials explained that the Giroldi coup attempt failed these tests. But in so explaining the refusal of the United States fully to back the insurrection, the Bush administration effectively set conditions for future intervention that challenged established legal norms, particularly those that prohibit the use of force to change a nation's government because of its allegedly illegitimate character.[34] Bush reportedly signed an intelligence finding to expend $3 million on the planning of a coup in Panama, this time benefiting from more American control.[35] Yet, with only slight adjustment, the criteria established to support an internal coup in Panama would serve well the objectives of the massive and overt U.S. invasion less than three months later, despite the absence of any indigenous coup at that time.

The second question to arise from the Giroldi coup attempt was whether the U.S. government may assist in the launching of a coup if the strong possibility exists that a government leader will be assassinated or otherwise killed during the coup. Executive order 12333, which President Reagan signed in 1981, prohibits assassinations of foreign officials.[36] The Bush Justice Department reportedly introduced a new interpretation of that order, which held that the ban on assassinations does not prevent U.S. assistance to indigenous coup leaders when there is reason to believe that their attempt to seize control of the government may lead to the death of government officials.[37]

Third, would the extraterritorial reach of U.S. criminal law empower U.S. law enforcement agencies and armed forces to seize alleged criminals in foreign countries without the knowledge or permission of local authorities? In two legal memoranda the Justice Department reportedly concluded that the Federal Bureau of Investigation and the U.S. armed forces can legally seize fugitives in other countries under such circumstances, even though such arrests may contravene restrictions found in customary international law.[38] The State Department legal adviser also argued, in supporting the FBI's domestic legal authority to make nonconsensual arrests of fugitives abroad, that the "threats of some drug traffickers may be so serious and so damaging as to give rise to the right to resort to self-defense." Hence, arrests of this character could be regarded as legitimate acts of self-defense.[39]

What emerged from these events was the bare outline of a policy of intervention that differed from its predecessor, the Reagan Doctrine. The Bush policy appeared to endorse direct and indirect military intervention to promote democracy in totalitarian states and to combat international lawlessness. The administration did not conceive this policy as a reciprocal response to Soviet intervention. Rather, its target was thugs in high places, but only those thugs posing a threat to U.S. national interest. In some respects the Bush policy presents a greater challenge to international law than did the Reagan Doctrine. The latter at least pegged its legitimacy on the right to counterintervene against an external power—the Soviet Union—providing armed assistance to an oppressive government. The Bush policy offers no pretense of counterintervention. By the fall of 1989 it had evolved as a two-pronged policy: one aim was to remove a rogue leader, whether indirectly—by military coup, with its high, but acceptable, risk of assassination of government leaders—or directly—by the massive deployment of U.S. armed forces with orders to capture government leaders. The second

117

aim was to promote democracy by force of unilateral military intervention against an "illegitimate" regime.

Washington chose the direct route in late December 1989, sending 14,000 U.S. armed forces to invade Panama in Operation Just Cause. As described by Bush administration officials in its early hours and days, the operation sought to achieve four objectives: to protect American lives, to restore the democratic process, to preserve the integrity of the Panama Canal treaties, and to apprehend Noriega.[40] None of these objectives survives legal scrutiny with much credibility, a result that became increasingly evident as the facts about the operation belied the administration's characterizations of them. Official statements revealed a jumble of legal rationales and vague generalities to justify the military intervention.

The administration premised the first objective—to defend American lives—on hundreds of cases of harassment by the PDF during 1988 and 1989 and, more directly, on the fatal shooting of U.S. Marine First Lieutenant Robert Paz (who was unarmed but fleeing from a PDF roadblock), the beating of a navy officer, and the sexual intimidation of his wife over the weekend immediately preceding the invasion.[41] Henkin reminds us that the international law community accepts a limited right to intervene for the humanitarian purpose of rescuing individuals whose lives are endangered and where the local authorities are unable or unwilling to protect them.[42] As threatening as the PDF actions were, only a policy in search of a pretext for an invasion would interpret the incidents of December 16–17 as constituting the kind of widespread threat to American lives that would legally justify a deployment on the scale—and with the purpose—of Operation Just Cause.[43] Alternatives short of a massive invasion (such as evacuating all Americans to U.S. bases in Panama, lowering significantly the number of personnel and families living outside the bases, or removing many Americans from Panama) could have achieved Bush's first objective. A more limited U.S. military intervention might have been justified if it had met the tests of proportionality and necessity international law demands, namely, only to evacuate Americans from areas of danger and not to topple the ruling government.

The pronounced U.S. objective to restore the democratic process in Panama reflected the Bush policy's prodemocratic character and had enormous political appeal, both in the United States and among the Panamanian people.[44] Before the OAS, the U.S. representative offered a grandiose explanation that sought with its profundity to skate across the legal impediments:

> There are times in the life of men and of nations when history seems to take charge of events and to sweep all obstacles from its chosen path. At such moments, history appears to incarnate some great and irresistible principle, such as the nation-state in the 17th century, nationalism in the 19th century, and decolonization in the middle part of this century. Today we are once again living in historic times: A time when a great principle is spreading across the world like wildfire. That principle, as we all know, is the revolutionary idea that the people—not governments—are sovereign. . . . [This principle] has in this decade—and especially in this historic year 1989—acquired the force of historical necessity. . . . Democracy today is synonymous with legitimacy the world over; it is, in short, the universal value of our time.[45]

Missing from this eloquent interpretation of contemporary trends was the fundamental requirement that the legitimate creation of democratic societies arises from peaceful political evolution or violent internal rebellion. International law stops far short of empowering any nation to use military force to install or guarantee the success of democracy, or any other form of government, in another country. The International Court of Justice in the *Nicaragua* case rejected the Reagan Doctrine's rhetorical promotion of democracy—even in the guise of counterintervention—as a justification for the use of force.[46]

This limitation of international law does not deny the moral legitimacy of promoting democracy. But unilateral military interventions in the name of democracy or any other cause remain dangerous excursions into Pax Americana. If international law is to protect the territorial sovereignty and political independence of nations, it cannot sanction the violation of both in the name of democracy and still remain an internally consistent body of law. Perhaps some day operations to promote or protect democracy will have the approval of the United Nations or other relevant multilateral bodies, but that day has not yet arrived.

The third objective—to preserve the integrity of the Panama Canal treaties—might have offered a plausible legal justification for a limited military intervention if the canal in fact had been in real danger of sabotage or any other kind of attack by the PDF. The treaties authorize SOUTHCOM to use military force to meet the danger resulting from an armed attack or other actions that threaten the security of the canal. U.S. forces also are authorized to guarantee the security of themselves, their dependents, and their civilian components. If the canal's operations are interfered with, the United States can use military force to reopen it or restore its operations.[47]

Although the personal security of U.S. forces and American civilians outside U.S. bases in Panama was at some risk, nothing that occurred immediately prior to the U.S. invasion—including the killing of Lieutenant Paz—justified an invocation of treaty rights to launch Operation Just Cause. There was no armed attack threatened or under way against the canal; the PDF was not interfering with the canal's operations; and the security of American forces, dependents, and civilians on U.S. military bases in Panama was not seriously threatened.

Further, on December 15 Panama's National Assembly adopted what Washington would soon describe as a "declaration of war" against the United States. In fact, the declaration said that a "state of war" existed between the two countries because of the U.S. economic sanctions, which the National Assembly characterized as acts of "aggression."[48] The Bush administration initially found little reason to be concerned about the declaration.[49] Under modern international law, one state's declaration of war or of a state of war does not necessarily, by itself, trigger the right of self-defense by the target state.[50] The resolution acquired far more significance for the administration only after the killing of Lieutenant Paz and Bush's approval of Operation Just Cause on December 17.[51] But no hard evidence indicated that the National Assembly's declaration of December 15 threatened the security of the Panama Canal.

The fourth stated objective of the Panama invasion—to arrest Noriega—was politically irresistible. Noriega was a particularly noxious foreign leader and under indictment in the United States for facilitating drug smuggling operations. Bush was determined to apprehend him.[52] International law certainly does not prevent a federal grand jury from indicting a foreign leader, but it has a lot to say about how to bring individuals under indictment to justice when they are in a foreign jurisdiction.[53] Normally, an extradition treaty between two nations provides the legally acceptable mechanism by which to transfer alleged criminals from one sovereign jurisdiction to another. The United States and Panama are parties to such a bilateral treaty.[54] Not surprisingly, the United States could not employ the treaty against the very leader whose approval was required to implement it. Also, some question arose as to whether the Panamanian constitution permits extradition of a Panamanian citizen. Another method, which customary international law endorses, permits U.S. law enforcement agencies to pursue and apprehend a fugitive on foreign territory, provided the host government approves of such action.[55] Again, in Noriega's case, that approval was impossible to obtain.

Armed with the two legal memoranda of the Office of Legal Counsel in the Justice Department, which sanctioned nonconsensual arrests abroad by the FBI and by U.S. armed forces, Bush swept aside the international legal impediments to a search-and-seize venture against Noriega.

The Bush administration's four objectives were of a decidedly political character. Each embodied a perception of the national interest as the circumstances dictated. An overarching principle of international law, however, was needed to identify them as legally sound objectives; the administration relied chiefly upon the principle of self-defense to justify the political objectives, and then used the political objectives to explain the legal principle. A curious aggregation of disparate arguments evolved over the weeks following the invasion, casting doubt on both the objectives and the legal justifications.[56]

The inherent right of self-defense (qualified by the requirements of necessity, proportionality, and immediacy) arises under
international law in response to an aggressive armed attack or
the imminent threat of an aggressive armed attack upon the
defending nation or its armed forces.[57] Henkin describes how, in
the *Nicaragua* case, the International Court of Justice set down
some markers for what constitutes an armed attack and what
justifies the use of military force in self-defense.[58] As controversial as the Court's judgment proved to be, it offered a credible
standard against which to judge Noriega's personal conduct, the
numerous acts of harassment against U.S. nationals in Panama,
and the killing of Lieutenant Paz. Did these acts constitute an
"armed attack" on the United States giving rise to a right of self-
defense on the scale of Operation Just Cause?

Washington contended that U.S. actions in Panama during
Operation Just Cause were a legitimate exercise of the right of
self-defense. The administration invoked the self-defense provisions of the UN Charter (Article 51) and of the OAS Charter
(Article 21), and claimed it had exhausted all peaceful avenues.[59]
But rather than speak forthrightly of an armed attack against
the United States, U.S. officials spoke of the four objectives in
the language of self-defense: American lives had to be defended;
the democratic process had to be defended; the "integrity" of the
Panama Canal treaties had to be defended; America itself had to
be defended from Noriega.

This last claim proved particularly novel. Administration
officials described Noriega's alleged drug trafficking activities as
acts of "aggression" against the United States. Thomas Pickering, the U.S. permanent representative at the United Nations,
associated Noriega with "a war as deadly and as dangerous as any
fought with armies massed across borders" and went on to say
that "the survival of democratic nations is at stake."[60] The U.S.
representative to the OAS claimed that Noriega had

> declared war on my country a long time ago, from the moment he
> concluded his first deal with the narco-vermin who are wreaking
> havoc on our city streets and who seek to destroy our nation's most
> precious resource, its youth. Noriega and his ilk, whoever they are

and wherever they may be, are guilty of nothing less than premeditated aggression against my country.[61]

Deputy Secretary of State Lawrence Eagleburger labeled Noriega's alleged assistance to the cartels that shipped drugs into the United States and thus corrupted American youth an "intervention" in America's internal affairs. He warned that the United States would not tolerate any such intervention.[62]

These pregnant distortions of the language of international law—as attractive as they may have been to the American people—fell far short of the legal requirement for an armed attack giving rise to the right of self-defense. Drug trafficking across national borders remains a criminal activity demanding the targeted response of law enforcement agencies acting in accordance with established international criminal law procedures. Full-scale invasions to topple corrupt governments engaged in drug trafficking violate those procedures, regardless of whatever good may emerge from such use of force.

The U.S. invasion of Panama distorted the principle of self-defense. A political agenda that tolerated few of the limitations international law imposes upon even the most well-intentioned nations overtook the principle's central tenets—necessity, proportionality, and immediacy. It is not insignificant that few governments endorsed the American action.[63] At the United Nations, after the United States, the United Kingdom, and France blocked action in the Security Council, the General Assembly voted 75 to 20 on December 29, 1989, to condemn the U.S. invasion and demand a withdrawal of the invasion force.[64] The OAS found no legitimacy in the U.S. intervention and voted 20 to 1 to condemn it (the United States cast the dissenting vote).[65] The principle of nonintervention in the internal affairs of nations—which traditionally was viewed as being consistent with and protected by the right of self-defense—was repeatedly invoked in debates before these bodies.

Thus, as peaceful revolutions against communism were sweeping across Eastern Europe, the United States employed massive, direct, and unilateral use of its armed forces as the self-proclaimed enforcer of democracy and U.S. criminal law in the

Western Hemisphere. The events in Panama, including the rapid military success, the apprehension of Noriega, and the installation of the Endara government, restored American confidence in the use of force. But did it serve the national interest well? Some commentators have argued that reasoned adherence to international law serves the national interest.[66] In the case of Panama, it is very difficult to square the narrow political objectives of the U.S. action with the code of conduct among nations that international law represents.

The Bush policy on overt unilateral use of force eclipsed the Reagan Doctrine on covert unilateral use of force, but offered no superior claim to legitimacy. The far different response to the Iraqi invasion and occupation of Kuwait in August 1990 may well cast Operation Just Cause as a historical anomaly. But precedents of such significance as the U.S. invasion of Panama typically do not fade from the global political arena easily. In the future there no doubt will arise other lawless regimes whose conduct major powers like the United States find particularly threatening to their national interest or simply embarrassing. Whether international law holds firm in the face of more unilateral ventures or bends to conform to the political agendas of impatient governments remains to be seen. What is certain is that the rule of law remains at risk.

IRAQ

The Iraqi army's invasion and occupation of Kuwait in early August 1990 unleashed a process of profound importance to the future application of international law to military conflicts. One of the grand presumptions of the Cold War and of its progeny—the Truman Doctrine, the Brezhnev Doctrine, the Nixon Doctrine, the Carter Doctrine, the Reagan Doctrine, and unilateralism in general—was that the collective security system the drafters of the UN Charter envisaged was a reminder of their misguided and impotent idealism. Even those policies that gave birth to Operation Just Cause while the Soviet empire crumbled were premised on the irrelevance of collective security. For decades scholarship and statecraft about the legality of armed interventions centered on a nation's right unilaterally, or perhaps with a few other nations, to use military force. The "hard law" of the Charter—notably its prohibition of the use of force and its affirmation of the inherent right of self-defense—had been the touchstone of analysis and justification. The enforcement procedures outlined in Chapter VII of the Charter ("Action with Respect to Threats to the Peace, Breaches of the Peace, and Acts of Aggression") simply did not matter.

It took an atypical event of sufficient magnitude—namely, Iraq's invasion of Kuwait—as well as the end of the Cold War to activate the UN's collective security system. Even then, the Security Council could authorize only an ad hoc coalition of nations to take action against Iraq, an action that ideally should have been the responsibility of an organized UN armed force operating under Chapter VII as originally envisaged. Nonetheless, collective security acquired an identity and earned sufficient credibility to serve as an example for the future and to leave a deep impression on international law.

A limited treatment of this character cannot fully address the multitude of events and legal issues pertaining to the Gulf conflict.* Therefore, I have chosen six main categories of analysis, fully recognizing that topics omitted from this chapter deserve the prominence other scholars no doubt will accord them. Here we will focus on the following issues arising from the Gulf conflict:

- the tension between collective self-defense and collective security;

- the implementation of Chapter VII of the UN Charter during the Gulf conflict, including the imposition of non-military sanctions and the authorization to use force;

---

*By the term "Gulf conflict" I mean to encompass Operation Desert Shield and the crisis that continued between August 2, 1990, and January 16, 1991 (the "Gulf crisis"); Operation Desert Storm and the war that lasted from mid-January to late February 1991 (the "Gulf War"); and the immediate aftermath of the Gulf War, including the U.S. Operation Provide Comfort (the "Gulf aftermath").

- political rhetoric and the "just war";

- the modern application of the laws of war;

- humanitarian intervention; and

- war powers under the U.S. Constitution and UN Charter.

When one considers the enormity of the crimes the Iraqi government and military committed, as well as the unpredictability of how these legal issues—some quite novel—would be resolved, it is no small wonder that international law indeed was enforced during the perilous months of the Gulf conflict. It is also sobering to remember that while international law experienced something akin to a renaissance during the conflict, the Iraqi leadership seemed perpetually oblivious to the import of the rule of law. As one Pentagon official put it, it was as if Saddam Hussein awoke every morning and asked, "What international law shall I violate today?"

In the balance, however, international law was a winner during the Gulf conflict. Many nations galvanized their resources to defend the rule of law. In contrast, the isolated regime in Iraq never grasped the point of it all. Perhaps other rogue regimes in the future will miss the point as well and require equally determined, collective responses. But a powerful precedent has been established that should deter at least some of the aggressive stratagems of lawless rulers.

Collective Self-Defense and Collective Security

During the early stages of the Gulf conflict, Bush administration officials and others strongly advanced a theory that at any time following the Iraqi invasion of Kuwait on August 2, 1990, the United States was entitled under the principle of collective self-defense alone to use military force to enforce the trade sanctions the UN Security Council imposed on Iraq,[67] and to launch a counteroffensive against the Iraqi army occupying Kuwait and deployed in Iraq itself.[68] No explicit Security Council authorization would be required for either use of force. The final provision—Article 51—of Chapter VII of the UN Charter affirms "the inherent right of individual or collective self-defense if an armed attack occurs against a Member of the United Nations, until the Security Council has taken measures necessary to maintain international peace and security." All that was required, so the theory ran, was the request for assistance from the legitimate government of the victim state, Kuwait. And if the Iraqi army crossed into Saudi Arabia at any time, then U.S. forces deployed there under Operation Desert Shield would be entitled to use armed force against the aggressor under the right of both individual and collective self-defense.

No one would have credibly contested on legal grounds a U.S. counterattack against the Iraqi army if it had occurred immediately—within hours or days—following the invasion and if Kuwait or, if the circumstances required it, Saudi Arabia had requested such assistance. Nor would there have been any argument if the Iraqi army had invaded Saudi Arabia and coalition forces had acted in self-defense, even to the extent of liberating Kuwait and neutralizing the Iraqi threat to the region during the ensuing conflict. Article 51 clearly permits rapid unilateral or collective responses to aggression without waiting for a Security Council decision.

The principle of self-defense has been well honed over the centuries and thus leaves an impressive legacy compared with the largely untested principles of collective security Chapter VII also embodies. That is why Article 51 so pointedly reaffirms the "inherent right of individual or collective self-defense." But since the adoption of the Charter, the principle of self-defense has not existed in a legal vacuum, even though some states may have relied upon it as if it did. The UN collective security system, as envisaged in Chapter VII, is an organized means of exercising the right of collective self-defense, but in accordance with the Security Council's timetable and strategy. If nations could unilaterally defy the Council's decisions and engage in their own collective self-defense actions, then little would be left of a viable collective security system.

When the Security Council is actively seised with a matter and the procedural measures set out in Chapter VII are being implemented—until the Gulf conflict a rare event indeed—the collective security system cannot be ignored in deference to some unilateral action (particularly by a permanent member of the Security Council) taken pursuant to a claimed right of collective self-defense. An act of collective self-defense may conflict with the enforcement strategy and actions the Security Council has approved and implemented. If, for example, the United States had launched a counteroffensive against the Iraqi army in October 1990 without Security Council authorization, the economic sanctions and arms embargo the Council imposed upon Iraq to pressure it to withdraw from Kuwait peacefully and thus avoid armed conflict would have been fatally compromised. The Council's strategy was a step-by-step squeeze on Iraq, including a flurry of diplomatic initiatives, to obtain a peaceful resolution of the crisis. When the Council finally authorized the use of military force in the event Iraq had not complied with its relevant resolutions by a certain date (January 15, 1991),[69] it had reached the determination that those member-states capable of carrying out the will of the Council and willing to do so at their own discretion *after* the deadline should take the final step under Chapter VII.

In contrast, a failure of the collective security system is a failure to implement the principle of self-defense on the kind of institutionalized, collective basis the framers of the UN Charter envisaged. I have written elsewhere:

> If and when collective security fails, then there certainly arises, or more likely reappears, a legitimate basis for relying upon the inherent right of collective self-defense affirmed in Article 51 of the Charter. . . . It would be futile to define the point where sole reliance upon collective security can be legally abandoned in favor of sole reliance upon the right of collective self-defense. But this imprecision in international law does not deny the legitimacy of the distinction. The Iraq-Kuwait crisis at least established the important precedent that collective security can be implemented within a reasonable period of time.[70]

Notwithstanding their official positions to the contrary, the American and British governments bowed to political pressures in August 1990 and agreed to obtain Security Council authorization to enforce the trade embargo against shipping to and from Iraq with military firepower if necessary.[71]

Likewise, until early November 1990 both governments argued that a formal Security Council resolution authorizing the use of force to liberate Kuwait was unnecessary and would not be sought.[72] Again, political realities, if not strong legal arguments, persuaded both permanent members to seek the authorization. Once it was obtained with the adoption of Resolution 678 on November 29, 1990, each government relied upon that resolution—not collective self-defense—to justify both the threat and, beginning on January 16, 1991, the execution of the counteroffensive military campaign that quickly defeated the Iraqi army and devastated Iraq's infrastructure.[73]

This distinction between collective self-defense and collective security, and the policy implications it visited upon the U.S. and British governments, is not an international lawyer's attempt at legal hairsplitting. It goes to the heart of state policy and how and when a nation can apply its military force in the defense of another nation ravaged by aggression, particularly if in fact we are entering a "new world order." Following the collective security route during the Gulf conflict carried abundant political advantage. The Security Council authorizations were critical in holding the anti-Iraq coalition together, in providing the political (not to mention legal) legitimacy to the enterprise that solidified support among almost all member-states of the United Nations, and in substantiating the "just war" character of the coalition's military actions. Without them, well-meaning invocations of the principle of collective self-defense would have rung hollow within the Security Council chamber and the General Assembly as member-states rushed to condemn the precipitous actions of the powerful few. In the future, the United States would have struggled, perhaps futilely, to build another coalition to repel another rogue leader's blatant act of aggression. Instead, the precedents the Security Council established during the Gulf conflict establish the credibility of, and should enhance governments' reliance upon, the UN collective security system.

Implementation of Chapter VII Enforcement Actions

Thirteen of the fifteen Security Council resolutions pertaining to Iraq between August 2, 1990, and April 5, 1991, were explicitly adopted as UN enforcement measures under that musty chapter of the Charter (VII) that was supposed to ensure the maintenance of international peace and security following World War II. Only on a few occasions in the past had the Security Council invoked Chapter VII either directly or by inference to try to enforce its own decisions.[74] In none of those cases did the Council's action match the scale, frequency, or comprehensive character of the Iraq resolutions of 1990 and 1991.

The resolutions followed, up to a point, the step-by-step procedures set forth in Chapter VII. The Security Council determined that a breach of international peace and security had occurred, demanded Iraq's immediate and unconditional withdrawal from Kuwait, and called for immediate negotiations between Iraq and Kuwait to resolve their differences.[75] When Iraq ignored those requests, the Council adopted within a matter of days comprehensive trade and financial sanctions against Iraq and occupied Kuwait, and established a special committee to administer the sanctions.[76] A few weeks later, on August 25, 1990, the Council authorized the use of minimal force "to halt all inward and outward maritime shipping in order to inspect and verify their cargoes and destinations" and to enforce the trade sanctions.[77] A further resolution, adopted on September 25, confirmed that the trade sanctions applied to all means of transport, including aircraft, and required all states to enforce the Council's detailed directions against air traffic to and from Iraq and occupied Kuwait.[78] On November 29, the Council adopted Resolution 678, which established the deadline of January 15, 1991, for Iraq's full implementation of all relevant Security Council resolutions, failing which the coalition states were authorized "to use all necessary means" (implicitly meaning military force if necessary) to liberate Kuwait, to ensure Iraqi compliance with the resolutions, and "to restore international peace and security in the area."

These particular resolutions reflected the graduated pattern of enforcement set out in Chapter VII. The first step was a determination of a breach of the peace explicitly arrived at under Article 39. The second step required nonmilitary sanctions (as described by Article 41). The third step authorized the use of force to enforce the maritime trade embargo, and the fourth authorized the use of force to liberate Kuwait. The last two steps logically would be considered Article 42 enforcement measures, but the Security Council never designated them as such and, in fact, never specifically invoked Article 41 in establishing the sanctions regime against Iraq. Rather, a general reference to Chapter VII preceded each of these resolutions.

For international lawyers, these general references to Chapter VII generate debate over whether Article 42, in particular, was activated and, if so, whether the subsequent articles of Chapter VII must then come into play. For example, under Article 43 member-states should have entered into "special agreements" with the United Nations after World War II so that certain numbers of their respective national forces would be "on call" to the Security Council for enforcement actions ordered under Article 42. No such agreements were ever concluded, and therefore the Council has no troops at its immediate disposal to confront aggressor nations.[79]

In the absence of Article 43 special agreements, the Security Council would act under very questionable authority if it directed a member-state, whether under Article 42 or generally under Chapter VII, to use military force against another state. But Article 42 does not prevent the Security Council from *authorizing* member-states, such as the coalition governments in the Gulf conflict, to deploy their military forces, at their discretion, to enforce the Council's resolutions against a violator nation. Article 42 offers the Security Council wide latitude to determine that nonmilitary actions taken under Article 41 "*would be inadequate* or have proved to be inadequate" (emphasis added), and to "take such action by air, sea, or land forces [of Members of the United Nations] as may be necessary to maintain or restore

131

international peace and security." At the Council's discretion, it can authorize or direct that action.

Articles 45–47 of Chapter VII, which describe the workings of the Military Staff Committee (MSC), were premised on the anticipated conclusion of Article 43 agreements that would make national forces available to the Security Council. Again, without those agreements, the MSC could do little during the Gulf conflict. In any event, the MSC serves at the pleasure of the Security Council. Its primary role is to assist in the Council's plans for the application of armed force. Even where forces are placed at the Council's disposal, the MSC would not necessarily "command" those forces. In the Gulf conflict, the Security Council remained silent on the issue of military command of forces authorized to enforce the Council resolutions. The Charter thus is flexible enough—both with respect to the Security Council's decision to authorize the use of military force and regarding the command of the forces used under that authority—to have served the Security Council well during the Gulf conflict.

Other resolutions adopted prior to Resolution 678 encompassed a wide range of demands and nonmilitary actions aimed at restoring international peace and security. These resolutions achieved the following:

- nullified Iraq's annexation of Kuwait,[80]

- demanded the immediate departure of foreign nationals,[81]

- demanded full privileges, including immunity, for diplomats in occupied Kuwait and the rescission of orders to close diplomatic premises,[82]

- established a procedure for provision of humanitarian foodstuffs and medical supplies to Iraq and occupied Kuwait,[83]

- further demanded the protection of diplomatic personnel and premises in occupied Kuwait and in Iraq,[84]

- authorized the sanctions committee to examine requests from states suffering economic hardship related to implementation of the trade sanctions against Iraq, and to recommend appropriate action,[85]

132

- reaffirmed that the Iraqi government and relevant Iraqi officials are liable for any violations of Geneva Convention IV of 1949 (Protection of Civilians in Time of War),[86]

- reminded Iraq of its liability under international law for losses, damages, and injuries inflicted upon Kuwait and other countries and their nationals and corporations,[87] and

- invited states to collect relevant information regarding the various claims against Iraq.[88]

Iraq's continuing noncompliance with these resolutions provided additional grounds for the military enforcement action Resolution 678 authorized. Thus the coalition governments had authorization not only to reverse Iraq's aggression against and occupation of Kuwait, but also to ensure that Iraq fully complied with all of the resolutions pertaining to the consequences of that aggression and occupation. This was an extraordinary application of Chapter VII's military enforcement powers, for it confirmed the use of force under UN authority as a legitimate means to correct violations of international law that are related to but are not themselves acts of aggression.

Chapter VII's extended application became apparent when the Security Council addressed the aftermath of the Gulf War. The Council adopted Resolution 687 of April 3, 1991—which set forth in thirty-four operative paragraphs the cease-fire arrangements and obligations that Iraq would need to comply with following its defeat in the war—under Chapter VII. This enabled the Council to continue economic sanctions and the arms embargo against Iraq. The resolution provided that the coalition governments would maintain forces in southern Iraq until the completion of the deployment of a UN observer unit in a demilitarized zone along the Iraq-Kuwait border.[89]

Resolution 687's establishment of an intrusive UN inspection, verification, and arms destruction regime, and the creation of a UN fund to collect and pay compensation for claims arising from Iraq's invasion and occupation of Kuwait, clearly reflected the wide range of nonmilitary options available under Chapter VII. Because the Chapter VII umbrella already had covered and would continue to cover the entire Gulf conflict, including the aftermath of the war, any violation by Iraq of the mandatory, comprehensive arms control regime established by the Security Council could lead the Council to adopt further explicit military measures to ensure compliance.

Thus the implementation of Chapter VII nonmilitary measures against Iraq promised to become a multiyear exercise, one that could readily trigger an authorization to reemploy military force against Iraq if the circumstances warranted. For the first time in the history of the United Nations, one of its members remained perpetually, and one might argue statutorily, at risk of being disciplined with military force under Chapter VII to ensure compliance with highly intrusive Security Council resolutions.

Political Rhetoric and the "Just War"

Neither the UN Charter nor any other contemporary codification of international law refers to the "just war" or defines the conditions for one. A simple modern formula holds that the just war is one consistent with the UN Charter, while the unjust war is one conducted in violation of the Charter.[90] But that formula does not explain why Bush and others so passionately defended the Gulf War as a just war, even more than they did Operation Just Cause in Panama.[91] The appeal for a just war addressed concerns about the morality of Operation Desert Storm, particularly as the chosen alternative to continued economic sanctions. By invoking the rhetoric of the just war, Bush served vital political interests both at home and abroad. He had to distinguish the Gulf conflict from the murkier ones of the Cold War, because the massive American commitment in Operation Desert Shield, redoubled on November 8, 1990, was so purposeful that war (of a type not known since World War II) was becoming inevitable.

The American public could understand the moral premise of a just war far more readily than it could comprehend lofty statements about the need to enforce international law. The latter required explanations of rules and procedures of global conduct only vaguely familiar to some. International law had not fared well with political speech writers and pundits during the 1980s, and thus lacked sufficient credibility to clinch the political support Bush needed. Bush, in fact, would refer to international law frequently during the Gulf conflict, but he needed more on the hustings. Bold pronouncements of a just war evoked religious and politically virtuous imagery in Americans accustomed to thinking that their political system is superior to all others and that their collective morality can be joined with military force for just causes.

The old just war doctrine that once dominated the study of international law stretches back to imperial Rome, to Christian theology during the Middle Ages, and to the origins of international law itself.[92] The doctrine thus greatly influenced the evolution of rules governing the use of force. As it developed, the just war doctrine divided into two branches: *jus ad bellum,* or justice in resort to war; and *jus in bello,* or justice in waging war. The latter became well established as the laws of war and will be examined in the context of the Gulf War shortly. *Jus ad bellum* has a far less doctrinal character today, having been eclipsed by the UN Charter and modern secular principles about the nonuse of force and the right of self-defense. However, if political leaders insist on invoking the language of the just war, it behooves us to understand some of its fundamental principles—however dated—and to appreciate its considerable limitations in light of modern international law.

Jus ad bellum traditionally relied upon some ultimate authority to interpret and apply the various just causes involved in waging a war. One side is just; the other side is morally defenseless. This determination was plausible as long as the influence of natural law and theology (particularly the teachings and authority of the Catholic church) pervaded international legal scholarship. But with the growing secularization of international law by the eighteenth and nineteenth centuries, theories about the just war faced imponderable obstacles. One could find just causes on both sides of a conflict under modern international law, and modern law established no impartial, ultimate authority to render a final verdict on whose just cause was the worthiest. War itself was regarded as a legal undertaking; questions about the justice of waging it were relegated to other disciplines.

The Allied powers regarded both world wars as just wars, but did not invoke the traditional just war doctrine in making the claim. These global wars were just because the enemy was so threatening and indiscriminate in its aggressive behavior. Further, World War I was just because it would lead to the promotion of democracy and the decline of colonialism; World War II was just because it would lead to a new, more effective world order. In the meantime, the Kellogg-Briand Pact of 1928 outlawed aggressive war. The UN Charter in 1945 prohibited the use of force against the territorial integrity or political sovereignty of member-states except in instances of individual or collective self-defense or collective security. Thus the just war was limited to the strictly secular and limited options international law and, most particularly, the UN Charter afforded.

In recent times the only significant invocation of just war rhetoric was made by Soviet bloc and Third World countries supporting wars of national liberation for the "just cause" of self-determination. A great deal of political discourse (particularly at the United Nations) has been devoted to establishing the basis for a state's military intervention in support of a group in another country fighting a colonial government or otherwise pursuing its right of self-determination.[93] At the United Nations, the General Assembly awarded impressive legitimacy to such wars of national liberation in the Declaration on Principles of International Law concerning Friendly Relations and Co-operation among States in Accordance with the Charter of the United Nations (1970), Article 7 of the Resolution on the Definition of Aggression (1974), the Declaration on Strengthening International Security (1974), and the Declaration on the Enhancement of the Effectiveness of the Principle of Refraining from the Threat or Use of Force in International Relations (1987).

Michael Reisman of Yale Law School has written that an inversion occurred in international law with the adoption of these resolutions and the judgment of the International Court of

Justice in the *Nicaragua* case.[94] The traditional right under international law permitted military support to the ruling government where an internal insurgency (short of civil war) threatened the security of the state; under the new theory of just wars embodied in these documents, by contrast, it would be illegal to support the ruling government, but perfectly legal, perhaps obligatory, to provide military support to the national liberation movement.

The Gulf conflict, however, was an old-fashioned interstate war. If Iraq's blatant aggression against and occupation of Kuwait was to be reversed with the promise that a just war was in the offing, then what were the criteria typically associated with the so-called just wars of past centuries?

1. The cause must be just. In the classic paradigm the only just cause of modern times is self-defense. This certainly applied to Kuwait and, on a collective basis, to the United States and the coalition governments. However, a more expansive principle of self-defense has incorporated the classic notions of punishing evil and retaking what has been wrongly seized. In the Gulf conflict, under the aegis of self-defense, the coalition forces retook Kuwait and punished the "evil" regime of Saddam Hussein.

2. A lawful authority must decide to resort to force. This criterion requires that only the highest political authority in the state may decide upon using military force. Today the even higher authority of the UN Security Council can act as the lawful authority; it did so with passage of Resolution 678. In the United States, the Congress explicitly authorized Bush to take military action.

3. The intention must be right. Was the United States prepared to fight only to defend, and recapture in Kuwait, the vital oil resources of the Middle East, or was the U.S. intention to enforce international law? This question probably will remain debatable. The defense of Kuwait and Saudi Arabia and the fulfillment of the Security Council's mandate to reverse Iraq's aggression coincided with the obvious presence of oil in the region. Until a similar act of aggression occurs in a less economically vital area of the world and the United States acts with similar determination, the "war for oil" allegation will persist. In any event, going to war to defend the economic lifeline of significant sectors of the world economy may be a justifiable use of force, particularly when the Security Council authorizes it.

4. The use of force must be a last resort. This criterion was the driving force behind the early January 1991 congressional debate over whether to delay the counteroffensive until economic sanctions, as well as peace overtures, had had more time to show conclusively that Iraq would not withdraw under such pressure. What constitutes the "last resort" is a matter of judgment. Prolonging the standoff with Iraq would have entailed more suffering by Kuwait and Iraqi civilians and permitted Saddam Hussein to further consolidate his gains. In light of the deadline the Security Council established, and the futile negotiations Secretary of State James Baker[95] and UN Secretary-General Javier Pérez de Cuéllar undertook just prior to that deadline,[96] one could make a reasonable case that efforts to find a peaceful resolution of the crisis had been exhausted.

5. The cost-benefit ratio must be convincing. In classic terms, this means that the good sought in the war must outweigh the evils the war would produce. In the final analysis, this may be the toughest criterion for the United States to satisfy. The coalition forces achieved the objective of the Gulf War—to liberate Kuwait—and crippled the Iraqi army as an offensive force. But the costs were high. First, the unprecedented environmental damage the war inflicted, particularly oil pollution in the Persian Gulf and the torching of over 700 oil wells in Kuwait, may constitute a long-term environmental disaster for that region and may have an unpredictable impact on the world's ozone layer and climate.[97]

Second, the internal aggression the Iraqi army unleashed on the Kurdish and Shiite minorities may have caused thousands of casualties and it precipitated the largest exodus of refugees and displaced persons in the shortest span of time in modern history. Thousands more may have died from the hardships of their flight to the Turkish, Iranian, and Kuwaiti borders. The Iraqi army reportedly plundered the homes and personal property the refugees left behind. The refugees' precarious situations, particularly in Iraq itself, promised continued risk for their security.

Third, coalition bombing during the war severely damaged the infrastructure of Iraq. In the aftermath of the war, the Iraqi civilian population suffered from the lack of electricity and, consequently, power to generate fresh water and treat sewage. Any evaluation of the war would have to weigh the bombing campaign and low coalition casualty count against the high cost of rebuilding Iraq's infrastructure and the large number of civilian deaths during the Gulf aftermath.

Fourth, the number of Iraqi troops killed during the war may have exceeded 100,000; a reasonably precise count may never be known. This is one of the most sobering costs of the war, one that raises important moral questions.[98]

6. The expectation of victory for just aims must be reasonable. The coalition governments were confident that their forces ultimately would prevail over the Iraqi army, particularly as the bombing campaign showed its devastating results. The number of casualties the coalition suffered and the duration of the fighting were much smaller than originally anticipated. The military campaign bore out the official expectations of victory, and therefore this criterion was satisfied.

7. The methods of war must be legitimate and proportionate. Modern warfare presents a paradox between devastating weapons and their technological wizardry. The total destructive capability of modern weaponry can prove decisive, as it did for the coalition forces arrayed against Iraq. That firepower can be very precisely delivered on target, thanks to modern technology. In a sense, "smart bombs" make for smart law, for they allow a belligerent to attack a military target located within a civilian area without causing "collateral damage" among civilians or of their property. The narrow test of customary international humanitarian law thus is met.[99] But smart bombs encourage military strategists to target a larger number of facilities that are essential to civilian needs, even if they may also facilitate military operations of the enemy. If a smart bomb misses its target, or is so powerful in its explosive capacity that even a direct hit inflicts brutally unnecessary damage, the risk of unintended but enormous civilian injury and damage arises in circumstances that might not have been entertained in earlier times.[100]

Until all the evidence of the bombing and ground war can be evaluated, the legality of all aspects of the coalition bombing campaign—including whether it was a proportional response to the risk the Iraqi army posed—will remain subject to question. The severity and magnitude of the destruction wrought upon Iraq and its army raise concerns about the legitimacy of the military strategy. Whatever the final verdict on the bombing campaign, when Bush ordered an end to the fighting on February 27, 1991, while the Iraqi army was in frantic retreat from Kuwait, he acted in recognition of the limits international law imposes on the conduct of warfare.

These classic criteria for a just war are instructive, but they do not account well for a workable collective security system. Chapter VII of the UN Charter is structured to deal with "any threat to the peace, breach of the peace, or act of aggression" in a manner that may or may not involve the use of military force. The Security Council can tailor a nonmilitary or military response to political requirements without having to run down the just war checklist. A threat to the peace may not pass the classic test for a just cause. Whatever the Security Council recommends, authorizes, or decides is nominally lawful regardless of its merit. The Council's collective intention may be unfathomable. The Council may decide to use force long before force would otherwise come into play as a last resort. The consequences of UN-authorized military action may be more damaging than the initial act of aggression, and yet be a legitimate undertaking. The

Security Council has approved military actions, such as the Korean deployment in the summer of 1950, that did not promise, or ever deliver, victory in the classical sense. The means the Council legally approves may be disproportionate to the threat or breach to the peace or act of aggression, but approved nonetheless because that is what is required to maintain or restore international peace and security.

If there is a distinction to be drawn between the classic just war doctrine and the just war notions advanced during the Gulf conflict, it would be that the former legitimized unilateral action to enforce a religiously conceived morality, whereas the latter justifies multilateral action to enforce a secular international law. But in the age of the UN Charter, the many legal infirmities of a modern just war must temper its political appeal.

The Modern Application of the Laws of War

The laws of war, or *jus in bello,* played a central role in the Gulf War. They established the ground rules for the bombing campaign, Iraq's custody of civilian hostages, the treatment of both coalition and Iraqi prisoners of war, the Iraqi occupation of Kuwait and the subsequent U.S. occupation of southern Iraq, the timing of the cessation of hostilities, the care of the wounded in battle, and the accounting of dead soldiers. The Gulf War was the most significant test of the laws of war since World War II. Because the four Geneva Conventions of 1949[101] and the Geneva Protocols of 1977[102] had further codified so many of those laws, the body of international humanitarian law that nations should honor during times of war or lesser armed conflicts is now substantial.

The record of Iraqi compliance with the laws of war, examined in the immediate aftermath of the Gulf War, was dismal. Examples of Iraq's conduct include the following:

- the detention of foreign hostages in Iraq as "human shields," both during the early months of the Gulf crisis and in the final days of the war, when thousands of Kuwaitis were abducted and driven north with retreating Iraqi forces;

- the placement of military targets within civilian areas and the movement of civilians to military targets;

- the mistreatment, torture, and murder of Kuwaiti citizens;

- the looting of Kuwait, including the theft of cultural and personal property;

- the dismantlement of the administration of Kuwaiti law and of Kuwaiti government agencies, the destruction of Kuwaiti demographic records, and the imposition of Iraqi law and administration of all aspects of life in Kuwait; and

- the mistreatment of prisoners of war from the coalition forces, including televised interrogations.

The Iraqi mistreatment of foreign diplomats and the forced closure of foreign embassies in Kuwait City also violated conventions normally not associated with the laws of war but certainly applicable during times of war.[103] The Security Council reaffirmed in Resolution 670 that Geneva Convention IV applied to Kuwait and that Iraq was bound to comply fully with its terms "and, in particular, is liable under the Convention in respect of the grave breaches committed by it, as are individuals who commit or order the commission of grave breaches."[104]

Despite the wide reach of the laws of war, the Gulf War revealed disturbing gaps that will require greater attention by governments and international lawyers in the future. Iraqi authorities may have been responsible for the massive discharge of crude oil into the Persian Gulf, beginning in late January 1991.[105] The Iraqi army undoubtedly was responsible for torching over 700 oil wells in Kuwait during the war.[106] Were these acts violations of the laws of war?

Article 53 of Geneva Convention IV of 1949, to which Iraq is a party, prohibits the occupying power (Iraq) from destroying any real or personal property belonging to private individuals or the state unless for reasons of military necessity. More explicit reference to the environment appears in Article 35(3) of Geneva Protocol I of 1977, which prohibits employing "methods or means of warfare which are intended, or may be expected, to cause widespread, long-term and severe damage to the natural environment." Neither Iraq nor Kuwait is party to this protocol. Use of the environment as a weapon of war is the focus of the 1977 UN Convention on the Prohibition of Military or Any Other Hostile Use of Environmental Modification Techniques. Parties to the convention undertake in Article I "not to engage in military or any other hostile use of environmental modification techniques having widespread, long-lasting or severe effects as the means of destruction, damage or injury to any other State Party." Although Iraq signed the convention, it never ratified it. Kuwait ratified the convention but filed a reservation that makes it binding only with respect to other parties to the treaty, thus on its face immunizing Iraq from the convention's reach.

None of these conventions, particularly the last one, have adequate enforcement provisions. The Gulf War starkly revealed that a more comprehensive and punitive international convention should cover both damage to the environment and the use of the environment as a weapon of war. In the meantime, the case will have to be made that the 1949 Geneva Convention IV incorporates crimes against the environment and that, despite Iraq's failure to ratify them, relevant provisions in other conventions reflect enforceable customary international law.

The laws of war also will need to be revisited with respect to modern weaponry, particularly the duties incumbent upon both belligerents in connection with aerial bombing and the use of ballistic missiles. For example, international law poorly regulates the use of smart bombs and laser technology. A critical need exists to examine the legality of various targets, including whether top military leaders can be the legitimate object of individual targeting, by either assassination or bombing. (Should any place where they are located be classified as a "command and control center" subject to attack?)

Laws alone will not prevent the commission of war crimes. A further deterrent would be an international criminal court with jurisdiction to adjudicate cases brought against individuals for violations of the laws of war, as well as other international crimes. The Gulf conflict stimulated some political interest from top government leaders in the creation of at least some sort of international criminal tribunal. The obstacles they encountered in planning war crimes trials after the Gulf War emphasized the need for such a court. The International Law Commission of the United Nations first considered the establishment of an international criminal court in the late 1940s. The General Assembly directed it to address the question afresh in 1989.[107] A major hurdle—the definition of aggression—fell in 1974 when the General Assembly adopted a resolution on the subject.[108] The next step will be the completion and adoption of a Code of Crimes against the Peace and Security of Mankind.[109]

Humanitarian Intervention

One of the long-standing disputes among members of the international law community is the legality of military intervention to stop human suffering within a nation's sovereign borders. Henkin and the traditionalists limit such humanitarian intervention to rescue individuals (typically nationals) whose lives are in danger and where the local government cannot or will not come to their aid, and not to respond to atrocities visited upon local populations.[110] Advocates of the broader view of humanitarian intervention have powerful examples to justify military intervention,[111] but have never convinced political leaders in general or the United Nations of the merit of their cause. In 1991 the traditionalist view still prevailed; international law granted no general right unilaterally to charge into another country to save its people from their own leaders.

Nonetheless, the immediate aftermath of the Gulf War challenged the narrow view of humanitarian intervention. The Iraqi army's campaign against the rebelling Kurds and Shiite peoples of Iraq drove an estimated two million of them north into Turkey, west into Iran, and south into the occupied zone of southern Iraq. Thousands of Kurds and Shiites reportedly were killed or wounded.[112] Many of the refugees bore the scars of Iraqi firepower. The refugees' mass destitution—many died each day from starvation, dehydration, disease, and exposure—and the

144

resistance of Turkey and, to a far lesser extent, Iran—long fearful of Kurdish insurgencies in their own states—to accept them as refugees or, when left with no choice, to do so only on a temporary basis, forced the issue of intervention upon the Security Council.

The Council responded by adopting, on April 5, 1991, Resolution 688, which established a right to interfere on Iraqi territory for humanitarian purposes.[113] The resolution merits close scrutiny, for while it was a milestone in the development of international law, it was not the great leap forward to military intervention for humanitarian purposes that some claimed it was within days of its adoption.[114]

Resolution 688 condemned the repression of the Iraqi civilian population and described its consequences as threats to international peace and security in the region, demanded an end to the repression and an opening of a political dialogue, and insisted "that Iraq allow immediate access by international humanitarian organizations to all those in need of assistance in all parts of Iraq and to make available all necessary facilities for their operations." It requested the UN secretary-general to use all the resources at his disposal to address "urgently the critical needs of the refugees and displaced Iraqi population." Then the Security Council appealed to all member-states and all humanitarian organizations to contribute to the humanitarian relief efforts the resolution described. The resolution demanded "that Iraq cooperate with the Secretary-General to these ends."

At the time Resolution 688 was under consideration, the Bush administration was seeking to avoid any military intervention in northern Iraq and was accelerating its withdrawal from southern Iraq.[115] The Council debate over the resolution indicated no intention that the resolution authorized any member-state unilaterally to move forces into northern Iraq. On the contrary, the discussion elicited reaffirmations of the principle of noninterference in the internal affairs of member-states.[116] Nor did a clear understanding arise that certain general wording in fact was code language for the use of force—as happened during consideration of Resolution 665 in August 1990 ("to use such measures commensurate to the specific circumstances as may be necessary") and Resolution 678 in November 1990 ("to use all necessary means").

Resolution 688 nonetheless established an important precedent. For the first time, the Security Council directed a member-state to stand aside and let international humanitarian agencies operate on its territory to assist citizens victimized by a government's repression. It stripped the Iraqi government of any right, under international law, to refuse admission to the humanitarian agencies. In fact, it obliged the government to make available "all necessary facilities for their operations." But the resolution did not strictly authorize the use of military force to achieve these objectives. Although Resolution 688 confirmed that the cross-border consequences of the situation were a threat to international peace and security, the Council purposely did not adopt it as a Chapter VII resolution. Even resolutions expressly invoking Chapter VII can be based upon threats to international peace and security without authorizing the use of military force. Rather, provisional measures or nonmilitary measures such as economic sanctions can be authorized. In the case of the Kurds, a further Council resolution would have been required to authorize military intervention for humanitarian purposes.

Events outpaced the Council when, within days of the adoption of Resolution 688, the American, British, and French governments argued that the resolution authorized their hastily planned military deployments in northern Iraq to create a *de facto* safe haven that would draw the Kurds back into their own country and in which the humanitarian agencies could operate safely.[117] The Kurds' plight, in particular, had become so vividly disastrous (thanks to television) that political pressures to intervene militarily had seized the moment.

But the allied deployment should not be regarded as a new type of lawful military intervention to stop a government's acts of repression and the consequent suffering of its own people. Indeed, the intervention was the right action but for the wrong reason. The Bush administration would have been more honest if it had invoked the broad view of humanitarian intervention—

146

controversial though it may be—or had argued that the UN Charter's prohibition of interference in the internal affairs of member-states, Article 2(7), is inapplicable where member-states are continuing to take enforcement measures under Chapter VII. The cease-fire resolution (687) is probably the most intrusive resolution in the United Nations' history, and its application under Chapter VII may persist for a long time.

Law here matters. The Kurdish exodus from Iraq demanded an immediate response. The need for the American and European intervention was critical under the circumstances. But the reasons invoked to use military force overseas are important, for they establish precedents, affect the way other governments and the United Nations react, and deeply influence the duration and magnitude of a nation's commitment.

The U.S. interpretation of Resolution 688 initially guided U.S. policy into a surprisingly wishful conception of the future: U.S. forces would be withdrawn within a short time, and a large number of international humanitarian workers would, in the words of Assistant Secretary of State John Bolton on May 9, "[deter] Saddam Hussein from conducting any reprisals against the refugees and displaced."[118]

The Bush administration denied on a number of occasions during the Gulf conflict the need to obtain Security Council authorization or action, only then to seek it, obtain it, and repeatedly rely upon it for legal justification of U.S. military operations.[119] The Kurdish debacle triggered a different strategy. On April 11, 1991, six days after the Security Council adopted Resolution 688 and five days before the first American soldiers entered northern Iraq, the Senate unanimously adopted a resolution proposed by Senator Daniel Patrick Moynihan that called upon the president to return to the Security Council to initiate enforcement actions under Chapter VII in order to end Iraq's repression of the Iraqi civilian population. The Senate recommended the Security Council consider the following measures:

(1) establishing temporary enclaves to provide sanctuary to those fleeing Iraqi troops, (2) developing procedures to verify the full implementation of any Iraqi Government offer of amnesty to Iraqi citizens, (3) maintaining economic sanctions against Iraq, and (4)

using effective means to protect refugees pursuant to Article 42 of
the United Nations Charter.[120]

The Moynihan resolution properly distinguished between the humanitarian relief character of Resolution 688 and the further action that the Security Council would need to take to authorize the use of armed force in northern Iraq to achieve humanitarian objectives.

The significance of the Moynihan resolution rested with its recognition of the additional steps necessary to protect the Kurds. Bush chose instead to interpret Resolution 688 as sufficient authority to intervene in northern Iraq. The responsibility fell upon the UN secretary-general to start deploying a UN "guard force" of up to 500 lightly armed troops in late May 1991 to serve as observers and provide some protection for UN relief workers within northern and eastern Iraq.[121] Nonetheless, no UN security force would be present to offer protection for Iraqi civilians within areas where UN humanitarian workers and the UN guard force were operating.

By July 15, U.S. and European forces had withdrawn from northern Iraq, and a small allied contingent, initially numbering about 2,500 soldiers, was stationed in southeastern Turkey. Allied troops were implicitly pledged to the defense of the Kurds in the former allied security zone in northern Iraq in the event the Iraqi army attacked, and thus were poised to launch a humanitarian intervention with or without Security Council authorization.

War Powers under the U.S. Constitution and UN Charter

It is not uncommon for theoretical discord to emerge from the marriage of international legal obligations with domestic constitutional requirements. Although the Bush administration argued that the United States did not require Security Council authorization to wage war against Iraq, it eventually recognized the value in obtaining that authorization. Once Security Council Resolution 678 was adopted on November 29, 1990, U.S. officials reiterated their other contention (held from the beginning of the Gulf crisis) that the administration did not require congressional

approval to launch a counteroffensive against the
Rather than invoke the principle of self-defense, ho
cials began to refer to Resolution 678 as an internatio
tion that the United States was bound to perform.[1]

It was a powerful, but curious, argument for the administration to use in the weeks preceding the Gulf War. Resolution 678
only authorized the use of all necessary means to liberate
Kuwait: the Security Council did not require or otherwise direct
the United States actually to launch the counteroffensive. Therefore, the United States was under no treaty obligation to take
military action at the request of the Security Council. The absence of any Article 43 special agreement between the United
States and the United Nations meant that the Security Council
had no legal authority to compel U.S. military intervention anywhere.[123]

As for the president's constitutional authority to enter the
war, the debate over the separation of war powers between the
president and the Congress had been waged for two centuries
and was not resolved during this particular episode in America's
foreign policy. But two factors—the president's insistence that he
did not require congressional approval for use of force but his
finally asking for it a few days before the Security Council's
deadline;[124] and the compelling need for the United States to
enforce international law, this time with the express authority of
the Security Council—exerted considerable pressure on Congress to reach the kind of decision it had so often shunned in the
past, namely, whether or not to commit the United States to war.

Following three days of debate on January 10–12, 1991, the
House of Representatives (in a 250–183 vote) and the Senate
(voting 52–47) approved a resolution authorizing the president
to use U.S. armed forces after January 15 to carry out what the
Security Council had authorized in Resolution 678. The debate
centered primarily on the choice between two measures: S.J. Res.
1 (H.Con. Res. 33), or the Nunn-Hamilton resolution, requiring
continuation of the Security Council's economic sanctions regime against Iraq until Congress made a further determination
to authorize the use of military force; and H.J. Res. 77 (S.J. Res.

2), or the Solarz-Fascell resolution, authorizing use of force after the Security Council deadline.[125]

The Nunn-Hamilton resolution was consistent with Security Council Resolution 678, which left all options open to the coalition once the January 15 deadline had passed. Both chambers voted it down, but that should not detract from the fact that, like the Solarz-Fascell resolution, it supported Chapter VII enforcement action. However, unlike the Solarz-Fascell resolution, the Nunn-Hamilton measure proposed two distinct stages of enforcement: a continuation of nonmilitary sanctions and then, if necessary, a further congressional determination of military intervention. If the Nunn-Hamilton resolution had become law and Congress had never authorized—and Bush had never launched—the American counteroffensive, the United States still would have remained in strict compliance with Resolution 678. The reason lies not only in the flexible language of Resolution 678 itself, but also in the original design for collective security conceived in 1945 when the Senate approved the resolution of ratification for the UN Charter[126] and both the Senate and the House passed the UN Participation Act.[127] That design for collective security reveals how intertwined are the requirements of the Charter and the Constitution.

One clear message emerged from the 1945 congressional hearings and debates about UN collective security: the president has no legal authority to launch a large-scale U.S. military intervention under UN authority—like Operation Desert Storm—without first obtaining congressional approval.[128] There would be no international legal obligation to participate in what one scholar has described as "wholesale war" sanctioned by the Security Council.[129] Rather, the U.S. government first would have to follow its domestic constitutional procedures. However, an international legal obligation to participate in UN "police" actions would arise, provided the United States had entered into an Article 43 special agreement with the United Nations.

Under the Charter regime the president can unilaterally instruct the U.S. delegate to the Security Council to vote in favor of military enforcement action.[130] The United States would be obligated to contribute armed forces to the Security Council to implement any such decision. But that obligation was to be met through what the U.S. Congress thought at the end of World War II would be swift negotiation and adoption of the special agreements called for in Article 43 and, in each case where the military intervention entailed more than a police action, further congressional authorization.

Few members of Congress in 1945 contested the president's frequent practice of ordering U.S. troops into action abroad without congressional approval to protect American lives and property, and even to enforce some treaty obligations. Congress agreed to preserve this prerogative of the president in connection with certain UN enforcement actions, namely, those international police actions ("skirmishes," as one senator described them) that the Security Council would order using the military forces committed by member-states under the special agreements. It seemed a sensible arrangement, because Congress would authorize a limited number of troops for such unforeseen contingencies when it approved the special agreement.

Congress anticipated attaching some reasonable conditions to the special agreement to protect against abuse of the designated U.S. forces by either the Security Council or the president. Where more is at stake, especially where the prospect of war eclipses what is available to the Security Council for police actions, Congress unreservedly believed that the commitment of additional U.S. troops would require its special approval and wrote that requirement into section 6 of the UN Participation Act.

The exclusive constitutional power of Congress to declare war remained intact. Members of Congress carefully distinguished between the Council's police powers and the war powers of Congress. Because most senators were so intent on granting the Security Council (and the president) freedom to use a limited number of U.S. troops for international police actions—a bold abdication of power that some senators believed inevitably would force the United States into war—they were doubly intent on preserving their constitutional power to commit American forces to larger conflicts.

Of course, much of what Congress debated in 1945 and contemplated as possible within the near future remained far ahead of the reality curve during the Gulf conflict of 1990–1991. In the absence of a special agreement, the president could derive no authority from the UN Charter to deploy any U.S. troops for a UN-authorized intervention of any size or character. Even if a special agreement between the United States and the United Nations had been in force when the Gulf conflict began, the president's exclusive authority would have been limited to deploying only that small proportion of the total U.S. armed forces the special agreement designated. Under those circumstances, a commitment of hundreds of thousands of U.S. troops to an enforcement action on the scale of a major war would require congressional approval.

History will view Bush's grudging request for congressional authorization as more significant than his attempt upon signing the Solarz-Fascell resolution to disclaim any constitutional responsibility to bow to the will of Congress.[131] The precedent of adherence to both international and domestic legal procedures in connection with a UN-authorized military intervention will remain to influence and guide future uses of force. The Solarz-Fascell resolution thus reaffirmed that the Congress has sometimes a constitutional duty to participate in the enforcement of international law, particularly when it involves U.S. armed forces.

THE NEW WORLD ORDER

Empire building, nationalism, and ideological zealotry commanded the armies of the past. What unifying theme will lead the armies of the future? Is it now possible to employ military might to enforce principles reflected in international law rather than to execute the strategic agendas of kings, dictators, and presidents? Is a modern just war plausible? The end of the Cold War presents an unprecedented opportunity to build a multilateral consensus on when military force can and should be used to enforce international law rather than defy it. For if a revitalized United Nations and emerging alliances of old adversaries are destined to manage peace in the new world order, these global enforcers must forge a modern compact on legitimate uses of armed force under the UN Charter.

For better or worse, the United States took the lead in creating a "new world order" in response to Iraq's aggression. The notion of a new world order, of course, was not new. Similar declarations were made after both world wars. In those cases the new world order that emerged was far different from that the victor nations envisaged. The League of Nations proved almost powerless when confronted with the aggressive juggernaut of the Axis powers. No international enforcement body intervened to stop the Holocaust, liberate Ethiopia or China, or repel Hitler's Panzer divisions. In the aftermath of another global conflict, the divisive politics of the Cold War strangled visions of a UN collective security system and of a world community committed to individual human rights.

What, then, is Bush's new world order, and is its future more hopeful than those of its predecessors? Bush has described the new world order as one "where brutality will go unrewarded and aggression will meet collective resistance."[132] It will be a "world where the rule of law supplants the rule of the jungle. A world in which nations recognize the shared responsibility for freedom and justice. A world where the strong respect the rights of the weak."[133] Bush has described the major elements of the new world order as being: "Peaceful settlements of disputes, solidarity against aggression, reduced and controlled arsenals and just treatment of all peoples."[134]

Thomas Pickering further articulated the premise of the new world order when he described "a new era of respect for international law, defended by a commitment to collective security." He continued:

> Underlying all of the factors which led to the success of the world's challenge of Saddam, there was an unbeatable partnership. This is a partnership without which there can be no enduring basis for peace and prosperity in the world. What I am speaking about is the partnership between the rule of law and the responsible applica-

tion of force. It is . . . that which gives us the right to say no, to say no to aggressors and to outlaws.[135]

Despite its susceptibility to varied interpretations, the partnership Pickering described is a powerful manifesto for a new world order, one that should not be underestimated.

Other new world orders also were predicated on confronting aggression and upholding the rule of law. They, too, were premised on optimistic judgments about the future ability of the world community to settle disputes peacefully within a multilateral framework. But the latest world order is unique in its primary emphasis on the use of collective military force to enforce international law. The new world order emerging from the Gulf conflict may achieve peaceful settlements of major disputes, but its focus is on the multilateral enforcement of international law.

However, before the United States marches too deeply into the unmapped territory of the new world order, the tension between Operation Just Cause and the collective security system (however fragile) employed in the Gulf conflict must be resolved. On the one hand, the policy that underpinned Operation Just Cause sanctions the unilateral application of military force to promote democracy and to arrest international outlaws. On the other hand, the "responsible application of force" that defines the new world order suggests collective decision making and collective military action.

To complicate further the mapping exercise for the new world order, the possibility remains that the Bush policy would be implemented to deal with a ruler like Saddam Hussein who survives a collective enforcement action, continues to violate international law (including the emerging crime of internal aggression), and denies his people democratic reform. Alternatively, where such a venture fails to achieve its objective, the UN Security Council might, in certain circumstances, be compelled to authorize a multilateral action if only to clean up the mess left by the unilateral effort's debacle.

The nucleus of the new world order is the determination of the world community to enforce international law. Operation

Just Cause did not serve that purpose well even though it may have espoused a moral purpose and served some law enforcement aims. It sought to enforce a highly selective bundle of international legal obligations bearing upon U.S. security and the U.S. criminal code. The new world order requires a far broader commitment to enforce international law even when the violation may not have a direct bearing upon the U.S. national interest, and a duty to resist unilateralism in favor of collective security measures.

The national interest, with its relatively parochial objectives, is too limiting for the tasks confronting the new world order. Policymakers will need to pay far more attention to what we might term the "global interest." Discovering that broader agenda, of course, will be no easier than efforts to fathom the national interest. But international law offers a starting point. Each of its rapidly multiplying principles establishes one common interest among nations. Together, these common interests constitute the global interest. As presumptuous as such an invocation may seem, the global interest can be advanced when international law is enforced. The collective response to Iraq's aggression showed some of the possibilities for enforcement actions.

But the Gulf conflict was an atypical crisis generating atypical responses. The new world order will face a wide range of political and military challenges of varying dimensions requiring an equally wide range of responses. Panama and the Gulf conflict reflect opposite ends of the spectrum. The more common threat to international peace and security will occur in murkier circumstances, where the national interest of the United States will either greatly influence U.S. policy or encourage apathy in the White House. Much more must be done to define legally sound means of responding militarily to these many types of threats.

Although it may prove useful again in the short term, the coalition-building exercise the United States led in the Gulf conflict is no model for the future. Collective security cannot be dependent upon a U.S. secretary of state's flying 100,000 miles over many long months to build the necessary coalition for an enforcement action. The major powers in the United Nations, as well as other member-states, must revisit Chapter VII of the UN Charter and negotiate modern variants of the special agreements called for under Article 43. The purpose would be to create a rapid deployment force, "on call" to the Security Council, that would respond to threats or acts of aggression immediately following an affirmative vote in the Council. Also, member-states should share more equitably the burden of military enforcement actions, as the framers of the Charter envisaged.

What should constitute legitimate uses of military force in the new world order? How should they conform with the "responsible application of force" Pickering describes? Two fundamental shifts in state practice must occur if the new world order is to realize its potential. First, unilateralism in the use of force must steadily erode in favor of collective actions, particularly those the Security Council authorizes. The Gulf conflict represented an initial move in this direction. Legal theorists and political strategists must focus less on justifying the unilateral actions of states by loading more exceptions on to the general prohibition of use of force, and focus more on what measures the United Nations and regional bodies could and should authorize to enforce international law. The growing list of unilateral military actions characterized during the 1980s as legitimate acts of self-defense will need to shrink to those armed responses that satisfy the conventional criteria of necessity, proportionality, and immediacy. The more unconventional the claim of self-defense, the more imperative it should become to take military action on a collective basis.

The second fundamental shift in state practice that must occur in the new world order is the replacement of ideological crusades to justify the use of force with the protection of the *collective* human rights of peoples who are suffering under repressive rule. To some degree, this shift is already under way. The Brezhnev and Reagan doctrines are no longer employed to justify superpower interventions. The right to interfere for strictly humanitarian purposes has taken an important first step in the wake of Security Council Resolution 688, despite the UN Charter's prohibition of interference in member-states' internal affairs.

The next step—namely, the right to intervene with military force to protect and facilitate those humanitarian purposes—has yet to take a firm hold in international law. It is a peculiar characteristic of international law that while intervention to rescue endangered nationals has enjoyed some legitimacy in international practice, intervention to save the lives of thousands or millions of people somehow fails the test of law. International law may yet evolve, particularly in relation to humanitarian interventions authorized by the Security Council. The easy case will be such interventions in support of or as a consequence of a broader Chapter VII enforcement action. The hard case will be where the mass violation of human rights is strictly internal, posing no real threat to international peace and security. Under those circumstances, not every atrocity will be stopped, because even on a collective basis, nations will decide in favor of preserving the sovereignty of the offending state if only to protect the principle of their own sovereignty.[136] As Senator Moynihan has cautioned, the future of international law need not include the abandonment of the Treaty of Westphalia.[137] But in the new world order some cases may well arise where collective military action is necessary to protect the collective human rights of peoples within their own borders. Otherwise, the new world order will simply perpetuate the illegalities of the status quo.

The whole notion of injecting legalisms—whether domestically or internationally—into the largely political decision of using armed force abroad always has been an uphill struggle. But it is worth the effort because the restraints, as well as the opportunities, that constitutional and international law present to political leaders will point toward the justification for their most difficult decisions. The Gulf conflict is a clear example. The first challenge in the new world order is to ensure that where the law requires restraint in the use of force, governments do not resort to false claims of self-defense to justify military interventions. Second, international law on the use of force already is evolving beyond the static presumptions of the Cold War and addressing violations of such fundamental (albeit sometimes conflicting) principles as territorial sovereignty and human rights. Collective action to enforce such principles, and to decide when one must yield to the other, will need to take precedence over unilateralism.

NOTES

1. Soviet President Mikhail Gorbachev pledged not to interfere with radical political reforms under way in Hungary and elsewhere in Eastern Europe during meetings with Hungarian party leader Karoly Grosz on March 23–24, 1989. See "Gorbachev Spurns the Use of Force in Eastern Europe," *Facts on File*: World News Digest with Index, vol. 49, no. 2524, April 7, 1989, pp. 243–244. On July 6, 1989, Gorbachev effectively renounced the Brezhnev Doctrine in an address before the twenty-three-nation Council of Europe. See "Gorbachev Spurns the Use of Force in Eastern Europe," *The New York Times*, July 7, 1989, p. 1.

2. See p. 29 of this volume.

3. Beginning in 1989, Soviet troops employed force against demonstrators in Lithuania, Georgia, and Azerbaijan. See, for example, "Moscow's Forces Step Up Pressure across Lithuania," *The New York Times*, March 24, 1990, p. A8; "Soviet Army Raids Lithuania Offices," *The New York Times*, January 12, 1991, p. A1; "Soviet Troops Seize Vilnius Phone Center," *The New York Times*, June 27, 1991, p. A31; "Soviets Report Use of Toxic Gas in Putting Down Strife in Georgia," *The New York Times*, April 20, 1989, p. A1; and "Troops seek to calm Azerbaijan; Soviets Debate cause of violence," *The New York Times*, January 18, 1990, p. A1.

4. See Lori Fisler Damrosch, "Constitutional Control of Military Actions: A Comparative Dimension," *American Journal of International Law*, vol. 85, no. 1 (1991), pp. 94–99; and "Shevardnadze Promises to Consult Parliament of Gulf Involvement," *The New York Times*, October 16, 1990, p. 18.

5. See, for example, "Five UN Powers Announce Accord on Cambodia War," *The New York Times*, September 10, 1990, p. 1; "Superpowers Seeking an Angola Agreement," *The New York Times*, September 17, 1990, p. 3; "Soviets Have Outlined a Peace Proposal for Afghanistan, U.S. Officials Say," *The New York Times*, July 15, 1990, p. 8. Although the United States and the Soviet Union engaged in serious dialogue on measures to settle the Afghan conflict, a stalemate in the superpower talks developed by 1991 for a variety of reasons. See Selig S. Harrison, "La lente implosion de l'Afghanistan," *le Monde diplomatique*, March 1991, p. 15.

6. See, for example, the Treaty on the Elimination of Intermediate-Range and Shorter Range Missiles, December 8, 1987, United States–Soviet Union, *International Legal Materials*, vol. 27 (1988), p. 84; the Agreement on the Destruction and Non-Production of Chemical Weapons and on

Measures to Facilitate the Multilateral Convention on Banning Chemical Weapons, June 1, 1990, United States–Soviet Union, *International Legal Materials,* vol. 29 (1990), p. 932; the Treaty on Conventional Armed Forces in Europe (CFE), November 19, 1990, *International Legal Materials,* vol. 30 (1991), p. 1; and the Charter of Paris for a New Europe, November 21, 1990, Conference on Security and Co-operation in Europe, *International Legal Materials,* vol. 30 (1991), p. 190.

7. Examples include cooperation in developing an agreement for submission to the compulsory jurisdiction of the International Court of Justice. See "2 Big Powers Back World Court Role," *The New York Times,* August 7, 1989, p. A5; and United Nations General Assembly Resolution 44/21, November 15, 1989, which was the first resolution the United States and the Soviet Union ever jointly sponsored in the UN General Assembly. The resolution reaffirmed the basic Charter principles and urged all states to "respect the principles of sovereign equality, political independence and territorial integrity of States and nonintervention in internal affairs, refrain from the threat or use of force inconsistent with the Charter, settle disputes peacefully, adhere to the principles of equal rights and self-determination of peoples, respect for human rights and fundamental freedoms, cooperation among States, and comply in good faith with their obligations assumed in accordance with the Charter."

8. "Baker Gives U.S. Approval If Soviets Act on Rumania," *The New York Times,* December 25, 1989, p. 13.

9. See David G. McCullough, *The Path between the Seas: The Creation of the Panama Canal,* 2nd ed. (Norwalk, Conn.: Easton Press, 1990).

10. Panama Canal Treaty, September 7, 1977, TIAS 10030.

11. Treaty Concerning the Permanent Neutrality and Operation of the Panama Canal, September 7, 1977, TIAS 10029.

12. Executive order 12635 (April 8, 1988), "Prohibiting Certain Transactions With Respect to Panama," *Public Papers of the Presidents of the United States: Ronald Reagan, 1988,* Book I (Washington, D.C.: U.S. Government Printing Office, 1990), pp. 425–427.

13. "Rift on Noriega Deepens As Bush and Treasury Chief Oppose Deal," *The New York Times,* May 23, 1988, p. 1; and "U.S. Abandons Effort to Persuade Noriega to Yield Power in Panama," *The New York Times,* May 26, 1988, p. 1.

14. "Soldiers Seize Tallies and Block Counting of Vote in Panama," *The New York Times,* May 9, 1989, p. A1; and "Effect Is Unclear—Electoral Panel Blames Foreign Interference in Presidential Vote," *The New York Times,* May 11, 1989, p. 1.

15. "3 Top Noriega Opponents Assaulted in a Street Melee," *The New York Times,* May 11, 1989, p. 1.

16. See, for example, President Bush's remarks quoted in "Bush Set to Extend Economic Sanctions Against Panama for a Year," *The New York Times,* April 6, 1989, p. 8.

17. President Bush announced this step and several others in response to the electoral fraud. See "Step Taken to Aid Ouster of Noriega," *The New York Times,* May 12, 1989, p. A1; "Transcript of President's Statement at White

House on the Crisis in Panama," *The New York Times,* May 12, 1989, p. A8; and "Bush Orders More Troops to Panama," *The Washington Post,* May 12, 1989, p. A1.

18. "U.S. Force in Panama Suggested," *The Miami Herald,* May 9, 1989, p. 1; and "U.S. Invasion Is Debated in Panama," *The New York Times,* May 16, 1989, p. A6.

19. Ibid. Senator Connie Mack (R.-Fla.) and Representative Gerald Solomon (R.-N.Y.) introduced identical legislation in their respective bodies urging the president to abrogate the Panama Canal treaties. See *Congressional Record,* 101st Cong., 1st Sess. (May 9, 1989), p. S5058 [S. Con. Res. 35], and *Congressional Record,* 101st Cong., 1st Sess. (May 10, 1989), pp. H1799, H1832 [H. Con. Res. 118]. See also "Canal Pacts: U.S. Looking at Dire Straits," *The New York Times,* May 10, 1989, p. A11.

20. "Bush Orders More Troops to Panama," *The Washington Post,* May 12, 1989, p. 1; and Press Conference with President George Bush and General Brent Scowcroft, National Security Adviser, Federal News Service transcript, May 11, 1989, p. 8-1.

21. "Remarks and a Question-and-Answer Session with Reporters on the Situation in Panama, May 11, 1989," *Public Papers of the Presidents of the United States: George Bush, 1989,* Book I (Washington, D.C.: U.S. Government Printing Office, 1990), pp. 536–537.

22. See p. 44 of this volume.

23. See David J. Scheffer, "Bush Chooses the Right Course in Panama," *The Miami Herald,* May 14, 1989, p. C1; U.S. Department of State, *Digest of United States Practice in International Law: 1978* (Washington, D.C., 1980), pp. 729–734 and 1027–1068; and U.S. Department of State, *Digest of United States Practice in International Law: 1977* (Washington, D.C., 1979), pp. 584–590.

24. "Bush Seeks Overthrow of Noriega," *The Washington Post,* May 14, 1989, p. 1; "Bush's Latin Gamble: Hoping Panamanian Armed Forces Will Oust Noriega," *The New York Times,* p. A3; and "U.S. Presses Effort to Oust Strongman," *The Washington Post,* September 1, 1989, p. 1.

25. I am indebted to my colleague at the Carnegie Endowment for International Peace, Viron P. Vaky, for his reflections on the role of the OAS during the summer of 1989. For background, see "OAS Calls for Power Transfer in Panama by Sept. 1, New Election," *The Washington Post,* July 21, 1989, p. A27; "U.S. Is Faulted on Military Maneuvers in Panama," *The New York Times,* August 24, 1989, p. A3; and "OAS Apparently Fails to Resolve Split over Measures to Remove Noriega," *The Washington Post,* August 24, 1989, p. A27. It is significant that two years later the members of the OAS unanimously adopted a resolution requiring the organization to meet in emergency session within ten days of a military coup in any member-state. The object of the session presumably would be to condemn the coup and possibly impose economic and diplomatic sanctions. See "Latin Nations Get a Firmer Grip on Their Destiny," *The New York Times,* June 9, 1991, section 4, p. 2.

26. State Department Regular Briefing, Federal News Service transcript, October 5, 1989, p. 10.

27. Press Conference by Secretary of Defense Dick Cheney, Federal News Service transcript, October 6, 1989, p. 2.

28. Ibid.

29. White House Regular Briefing, Federal News Service transcript, October 6, 1989, pp. 25, 30, and 33.

30. See, for example, ibid., p. 8.

31. The Bush administration encountered scathing criticism from Congress over its inability and unwillingness to provide adequate support to the Giroldi coup attempt. The congressional criticism pressured the administration to develop final plans for military intervention in Panama. See "Bush Aide and Senator Clash on Coup Attempt in Panama," *The New York Times*, October 9, 1989, p. 1; "Furor over Fiasco: It's Helms vs. the White House," *The New York Times*, October 12, 1989, p. A12; "Bush and Senators Meet on the Coup That Failed," *The New York Times*, October 12, 1989, p. A12; and "Bush Attacks Critics of Response to Coup," *The Washington Post*, October 14, 1989, p. 1.

32. Secretary of State James Baker on NBC's *Meet the Press*, Federal News Service transcript, October 8, 1989, p. 6.

33. Ibid., p. 1; Marlin Fitzwater, White House Press Briefing, Federal News Service transcript, October 16, 1989, p. 14-2; Marlin Fitzwater, White House Press Briefing, Federal News Service transcript, October 10, 1989, p. 11-1; Pete Williams, Department of Defense Press Briefing, Federal News Service transcript, October 10, 1989, p. 5-1; Richard Cheney, Department of Defense Press Conference, Federal News Service transcript, October 6, 1989, pp. 7–8; John Sununu on CNN's *Evans and Novak with Robert Novak and Fred Barnes*, Federal News Service transcript, October 7, 1989, p. 13.

34. Secretary of Defense Dick Cheney recognized the problem on CBS's *Face the Nation*, Federal News Service transcript, October 8, 1989, pp. 7–8.

35. "Bush Clears Plan to Topple Noriega," *The Washington Post*, November 17, 1989, p. A1; "U.S. Plans New Effort to Oust Noriega," *The New York Times*, November 17, 1989, p. A3.

36. Executive order 12333 of United States Intelligence Activities, December 4, 1981, 46 *Federal Register* 59941.

37. "Administration Alters Assassination Ban," *The Washington Post*, November 4, 1989, p. A1.

38. The first legal memorandum, dated June 21, 1989, pertains to the powers of the Federal Bureau of Investigation and partially reverses an opinion of the Office of Legal Counsel, U.S. Department of Justice, dated March 31, 1980. The latter opinion had determined that "U.S. agents have no law enforcement authority in another nation unless it is the product of that nation's consent," and that under its own general enabling statutes the FBI has no authority to make apprehensions in contravention of customary international law. The June 21, 1989, opinion of the Office of Legal Counsel concludes that the FBI's enabling statutes give it authority to "detect and prosecute crimes" and "make arrests" outside the United States and that the president has the authority to override restrictions found in customary international law, such as the requirement to

obtain a country's consent prior to an arrest on its territory by the FBI. See "FBI Authority to Seize Suspects Abroad," in U.S. Congress, House Committee on the Judiciary, *Hearing before the Subcommittee on Civil and Constitutional Rights,* 101st Cong., 1st Sess., November 8, 1989, no. 134 (1991), pp. 2–21. (For a reprint of the 1980 legal memorandum, see pp. 76–90); "Justice Dept. Says FBI Can Seize Fugitives Overseas," *The Washington Post,* November 9, 1989, p. A72; "U.S. Cites Right to Seize Fugitives Abroad," *The New York Times,* October 14, 1989, p. 3. In the second pertinent legal memorandum, dated November 3, 1989, the Office of Legal Counsel reportedly concludes that the Posse Comitatus Act of 1878, which prohibits the use of U.S. armed forces to enforce the law (such as make arrests) unless the Congress expressly authorizes it, does not apply outside the United States. Therefore, according to the Office of Legal Counsel, U.S. troops can be used to make arrests of fugitives, particularly terrorists and drug traffickers, in other countries. See "U.S. Military Given Foreign Arrest Powers," *The Washington Post,* December 16, 1989, p. A1. From memoranda of law filed by the U.S. attorney prosecuting Noriega in Miami, one can discern that the Justice Department relied heavily upon dubious case authority to support its contention of the Act's limited applicability. Further, even if the Posse Comitatus Act applies only domestically, the United States essentially argues that if the efforts of American law enforcement authorities are not likely to result in the apprehension of such alleged drug traffickers as Noriega and his collaborators, then the president unilaterally has the power to send U.S. troops into another sovereign country to enforce the laws of the United States and arrest such fugitives. Ignored in this process, of course, are U.S. constitutional and statutory law regarding war powers, international law regarding nonuse of force across national borders, and the customary requirement for host country consent to permit apprehension of alleged criminals. See David J. Scheffer, "The demons in the U.S. case against Noriega," *The Miami Herald,* February 11, 1990, p. V1.

39. The legal adviser also emphasized, however, the significant risks involved in pursuing a policy of nonconsensual arrests in other countries. See testimony of Legal Adviser Abraham D. Sofaer, U.S. Congress, House Committee on the Judiciary, *Hearing before the Subcommittee on Civil and Constitutional Rights,* supra note 38, pp. 22–24.

40. See "Situation 'Has Reached a Crisis,' " *The Washington Post,* December 20, 1989, p. A32; "Excerpts from Statement by Baker on U.S. Policy," *The New York Times,* December 21, 1989, p. A19. Addressing the nation on December 20, 1989, Bush emphasized the protection of American lives and the apprehension of Noriega as reasons for the invasion. See "Address to the Nation Announcing United States Military Action in Panama," *Public Papers of the President: George Bush, 1989,* Book II (Washington, D.C.: U.S. Government Printing Office, 1990), p. 1723. Secretary of Defense Dick Cheney chose to emphasize the safeguarding of American lives and the restoration of democracy to Panama. See "Excerpts from the Pentagon Briefing," *The Washington Post,* December 21, 1989, p. A38.

41. The State Department characterized the December 16, 1989, shooting of the marine as part of a pattern of "aggression" by Noriega. See "Panama Shooting Condemned by U.S.," *The New York Times,* December 18, 1989, p. A7.

42. See pp. 41–42 of this volume.

43. Bob Woodward describes how, following the aborted coup of early October 1989, the Bush administration developed detailed plans for various types of intervention in Panama, including a full-scale invasion to topple the Noriega regime. Training for an intervention had been under way continuously since early October. All that was needed was some provocative act to trigger a U.S. response. It is clear from Woodward's account, which Bush administration officials have not denied, that although some civilian advisers in the Pentagon questioned whether the killing of the U.S. marine was sufficient cause to justify military action, Bush's senior advisers found the incident unacceptable and employed it as the means to recommend launching Operation Just Cause. In a crucial meeting with Bush on December 17, 1989, his senior advisers, according to Woodward, presented only one option: a full-scale invasion that "would be a complete take-down of the PDF and the Panamanian government." It appears, from Woodward's account, that no legal counsel was present at this meeting and that legal issues were not discussed. (Attorney General Richard Thornburgh advised Bush on December 19, after Operation Just Cause had been authorized, that the United States had clear legal authority to undertake it. See "U.S. Cites Self-Defense; Legal Scholars Skeptical," *The Washington Post,* December 21, 1989, p. A36.) At the conclusion of the December 17 meeting, Bush authorized the launching of Operation Just Cause. See Bob Woodward, *The Commanders* (New York: Simon & Schuster, 1991), pp. 119–174. See also "U.S. Drafted Invasion Plan Weeks Ago," *The New York Times,* December 24, 1989, p. 1.

44. "Experts Say Special Circumstances Explain Strong Public Backing," *The Washington Post,* December 22, 1989, p. A33; "Panamanians in Ravaged Neighborhood Applaud the Invasion," *The Los Angeles Times,* December 26, 1989, p. A10; and "Critics of Invasion Still Hard to Find," *The Washington Post,* January 2, 1990, p. A8.

45. Statement of Luigi R. Einaudi, U.S. permanent representative to the OAS, before the OAS, Washington, D.C., December 21, 1989, reprinted in "Panama: A Just Cause," *U.S. Department of State Current Policy,* no. 1240 (1990).

46. Case concerning *Military and Paramilitary Activities in and against Nicaragua (Nicaragua v. United States of America),* Merits, 1986 ICJ REP. 14, pp. 130–134.

47. See Panama Canal Treaty, articles IV (1), IX (10); and Treaty Concerning the Permanent Neutrality and Operation of the Panama Canal, article IV and condition (1) set forth in the U.S. Senate's resolution of ratification adopted on March 16, 1978.

48. "Noriega Appointed 'Maximum Leader': Panama Says 'State of War' Exists with U.S.," *The Washington Post,* December 16, 1989, p. A21.

49. On December 16, 1989, Marlin Fitzwater, the White House spokesman, said that the declaration was "another hollow step in an attempt [by Noriega] to force his rule on the Panamanian people." He also confirmed that U.S. troops in Panama had not changed their alert status because of the declaration. See "Opposition Leader in Panama Rejects a Peace Offer from Noriega," *The New York Times,* December 17, 1989, p. A5; and Theodore Draper, "Did Noriega Declare War?" *New York Review of Books,* vol. 37, no. 5, (1990), p. 13.

50. Henkin writes of the December 15 declaration: "There was no declaration of war by Panama in any sense that traditional international law would recognize. . . . The [UN] Charter would permit the use of force by the target of a declaration of war only if the state declaring war also launched an armed attack." According to Henkin, "It is open to question whether a declaration of war, without more, qualifies even as a threat of force within the meaning of Article 2(4)." See "The Invasion of Panama under International Law: A Gross Violation," *Columbia Journal of Transnational Law,* vol. 29 (1991).

51. "U.S. Increases Panama Forces, Hinting Action," *The New York Times,* December 20, 1989, p. A1. Secretary of Defense Dick Cheney went so far as to characterize the December 15 declaration—coupled with the December 16 incident—as the most important factor leading to the invasion: "Obviously, we've tried for more than two years to resolve by peaceful means the difficult relationship that had developed with the government of Panama. This past week it came to a head with the declaration of Manuel Noriega as a maximum leader and his statement that a state of war existed between Panama and the United States." Quoted in "Excerpts from the Pentagon Briefing," *The Washington Post,* December 21, 1989, p. A38.

52. "Noriega Indicted by U.S. for Links to Illegal Drugs," *The New York Times,* February 6, 1988, p. A1. Once Operation Just Cause began, Bush repeatedly emphasized his objective of apprehending Noriega, and established a $1 million bounty for his capture. See *Public Papers of the Presidents: George Bush, 1989,* Book II (Washington, D.C.: U.S. Government Printing Office, 1990), pp. 1729–1731, 1739–1741, 1744, and 1749; "Doing the Inevitable: Bush Reportedly Felt that Noriega 'Was Thumbing His Nose at Him,' " *The New York Times,* December 24, 1989, p. A9; "Hunting Noriega: Tips, Bounty—and Frustration," *The Los Angeles Times,* December 22, 1989, p. A1.

53. See American Law Institute, *Restatement of the Law Third: The Foreign Relations Law of the United States,* vol. 1 (St. Paul: American Law Institute Publishers, 1987), secs. 431–433; M. Bassiouni, ed., *International Criminal Law: Procedure,* vol. 2 (Dobbs Ferry, N.Y.: Transnational Publishers, 1986).

54. Treaty between the United States of America and the Republic of Panama for the Extradition of Criminals, 1905, 34 Stat. 2851, Treaty Series 445.

55. See American Law Institute, *Restatement of the Law Third,* vol. 1, supra note 53, secs. 432 and 433.

56. The cacophony of rationales and principles was particularly evident in the State Department's cable of January 30, 1990, to all U.S. diplomatic and consular posts advising them of three legal justifications for the invasion. The first was the inherent right of self-defense "to protect [U.S.] forces and the 35,000 U.S. nationals in Panama from further attack." The cable offers the December 15 declaration of a state of war as evidence of the threat of use of force against Americans.

   The second justification centered on an exercise of rights granted under the Panama Canal Treaty in response to "escalating" threats and intimidation against U.S. nationals and those cooperating with them that "were making the efficient operation and defense of the Canal increasingly difficult." The cable noted intelligence reports indicating "that acts of sabotage against the Canal were contemplated." On December 20, 1989, Secretary of State Baker confirmed that "after the President had made his decision [to invade Panama], we received an intelligence report that General Noriega was considering launching an urban commando attack on American citizens in a residential neighborhood. I cannot prove to you that this report was absolutely reliable." ("Excerpts from Statement by Baker on U.S. Policy," *The New York Times*, December 21, 1989, p. A19.) Baker did not refer to a threat against the canal itself. Administration officials thereafter did not stress the threat of sabotage, casting doubt on its importance as a basis for the invasion, on the reliability of any supporting evidence, and on the characterization of the intelligence reports in the State Department cable.

   Third, the cable stated that "U.S. military operations in Panama have been undertaken with the complete support and cooperation of the legitimate government of Panama"—namely, the Endara government, which the United States installed just prior to the invasion. Thus, they "do not violate the principle stated in Article 2(4) of the UN Charter." The cable made no mention of Noriega's apprehension—the fourth political objective—or of any legal justification for it. See U.S. Department of State, "Panama: International Legal Justification," cable to all diplomatic and consular posts, January 30, 1990.

57. This definition, of course, attracts controversy. See Henkin, pp. 44–46 of this volume; Malcolm N. Shaw, *International Law*, 2nd ed. (Cambridge, Eng.: Grotius Publications Ltd., 1986), pp. 549–553; and Yoram Dinstein, *War, Aggression and Self-Defence* (Cambridge, Eng.: Grotius Publications Ltd., 1988), pp. 165–199.

58. See pp. 47–50 of this volume. Other scholars have viewed the court's judgment far more critically. See, for example, various contributions in Harold G. Maier, ed., "Appraisals of the ICJ's Decision: Nicaragua v. United States (Merits)," *American Journal of International Law*, vol. 81, no. 1 (1987), pp. 77–183; and Abraham D. Sofaer, "International Law and the Use of Force," *The National Interest*, no. 13 (Fall 1988), pp. 53–64.

59. Statement by Thomas R. Pickering, U.S. permanent representative to the United Nations, before the UN Security Council, December 20, 1989, reprinted in "Panama: A Just Cause," *U.S. Department of State Current Policy*, no. 1240 (1990); "U.S. Cites Self-Defense; Legal Scholars Skepti-

cal," *The Washington Post,* December 21, 1989, p. A36; "Administration Says International Agreements Support Its Action," *The New York Times,* December 21, 1989, p. A22; and U.S. Department of State, "Panama: International Legal Justification," supra note 56.

60. Pickering, ibid.
61. Einaudi, statement before OAS, supra note 45.
62. Lawrence Eagleburger on PBS's *MacNeil/Lehrer Newshour,* Federal News Service transcript, January 5, 1990, p. 6.
63. "World Criticism of U.S. Intervention Mounts," *The Washington Post,* December 22, 1989, p. A29; and "U.S. Denounced by Nations Touchy about Intervention," *The New York Times,* December 21, 1989, p. A24.
64. United Nations General Assembly Resolution 44/240 (December 29, 1989); and "U.S., Allies Veto UN Council Censure," *The Washington Post,* December 24, 1989, p. A16.
65. "OAS Votes to Censure U.S. for Intervention," *The Washington Post,* December 23, 1989, p. A7.
66. See, for example, Louis Henkin, *How Nations Behave,* 2nd ed. (New York: Columbia University Press, 1979), p. 331.
67. "American Blockade Is Criticized at UN," *The Washington Post,* August 14, 1990, p. A1; "U.S. Set to Enforce Embargo on Iraq," *The Washington Post,* August 13, 1990, p. A1; "Transcript of U.S. Statement About Measures Against Iraq," *The New York Times,* August 13, 1990, p. A11; and "UN Security Council Votes Embargo on Iraq; Saddam Says Seizure of Kuwait Is Permanent," *The Washington Post,* August 7, 1990, p. A1.
68. "U.S. Checks Allies on Use of Force," *The Washington Post,* November 4, 1990, p. A1; Abraham D. Sofaer, "Asking the UN Is Asking for Trouble," *The Wall Street Journal,* November 5, 1990, p. A14.
69. United Nations Document S/RES/678, November 29, 1990.
70. David J. Scheffer, "Commentary on Collective Security," in Lori Fisler Damrosch and David J. Scheffer, eds., *Law and Force in the New International Order* (Boulder, Colo.: Westview Press, 1991), p. 102. For similar views, see, in the same collection, Abram Chayes, "The Use of Force in the Persian Gulf"; Rein Mullerson, "Self-Defense in the Contemporary World"; and Oscar Schachter, "Authorized Uses of Force by the United Nations and Regional Organizations," especially pp. 77–79. The collection also includes a number of chapters representing contrasting views: see W. Michael Reisman, "Allocating Competences to Use Coercion in the Post–Cold War World: Practices, Conditions, and Prospects," especially pp. 42–44; Richard N. Gardner, "Commentary on the Law of Self-Defense," especially pp. 49–52; and David B. Rivkin, Jr., "Commentary on Aggression and Self-Defense."
71. See note 67; "U.S. May Seek Multinational Blockade Force," *The Washington Post,* August 7, 1990, p. A1; and United Nations Document S/RES/665, August 25, 1990.
72. See note 68; and "Baker Seen as a Balance to Bush on Crisis in Gulf," *The New York Times,* November 3, 1990, p. A1.
73. See "European Leaders Welcome News: But Unified Stand to Force Iraqi Pullout Pledged," *The Washington Post,* December 7, 1990, p. A30; State-

ment on the United Nations Security Council Resolution Authorizing the Use of Force against Iraq, November 29, 1990, *Weekly Compilation of Presidential Documents,* vol. 26, no. 48 (December 3, 1990), pp. 1947– 1948; The President's News Conference, November 30, 1990, *Weekly Compilation of Presidential Documents,* vol. 26, no. 48 (December 3, 1990), pp. 1948–1950; Message to Allied Nations on the Persian Gulf Crisis, January 8, 1991, *Weekly Compilation of Presidential Documents,* vol. 27, no. 2 (January 14, 1991), pp. 16–17; The President's News Conference, January 12, 1991, *Weekly Compilation of Presidential Documents,* vol. 27, no. 3 (January 21, 1991), pp. 39–43; Statement by Press Secretary Marlin Fitzwater on President Bush's Letter to President Saddam Hussein of Iraq, January 12, 1991, *Weekly Compilation of Presidential Documents,* vol. 27, no. 3 (January 21, 1991), pp. 43–44; Letter to Congressional Leaders on the Persian Gulf Conflict, January 18, 1991, *Weekly Compilation of Presidential Documents,* vol. 27, no. 3 (January 21, 1991), p. 59.

74. Examples include the Korean conflict (United Nations Document S/RES/83, June 27, 1950, and United Nations Document S/RES/84, July 7, 1950), Southern Rhodesia (United Nations Document S/RES/221, April 9, 1966, and United Nations Document S/RES/235, May 29, 1968), and South Africa (United Nations Document S/RES/418, November 4, 1977).

75. United Nations Document S/RES/660, August 2, 1990.

76. United Nations Document S/RES/661, August 6, 1990.

77. United Nations Document S/RES/665, August 25 1990.

78. United Nations Document S/RES/670, September 25, 1990.

79. The UN Military Staff Committee issued a report dated April 30, 1947, setting forth general principles for implementing Article 43, but the permanent members of the Security Council could not agree on certain aspects of the composition and organization of armed forces that would be committed under the special agreements. Nonetheless, the Council provisionally adopted many articles of the report in 1947. The text of the articles of the General Principles Governing the Organization of the Armed Forces Made Available to the Security Council by Member Nations of the United Nations, as amended by the Security Council, and an introductory note are published in United Nations, *Repertory of United Nations Practice,* Vol. 2, Articles 23–54 of the Charter (New York, 1955), pp. 393–408.

80. United Nations Document S/RES/662, August 9, 1990.

81. United Nations Document S/RES/664, August 18, 1990.

82. United Nations Document S/RES/667, September 16, 1990; and United Nations Document S/RES/674, October 29, 1990.

83. United Nations Document S/RES/666, September 13, 1990.

84. United Nations Document S/RES/667, September 16, 1990.

85. United Nations Document S/RES/669, September 24, 1990.

86. United Nations Document S/RES/670, September 25, 1990.

87. United Nations Document S/RES/674, October 29, 1990.

88. Ibid.

89. United Nations Document S/RES/687, April 3, 1991. U.S. forces withdrew completely from southern Iraq in early May 1991. See "Last G.I.'s Leave a Major Iraq-Kuwait Border Post," *The New York Times*, May 8, 1991, p. A16.

90. See Henkin, *How Nations Behave*, supra note 66, pp. 135–139.

91. Examples of Bush's use of the "just war" rationale include Remarks to the Reserve Officers Association, January 23, 1991, *Weekly Compilation of Presidential Documents*, vol. 27, no. 4 (January 28, 1991), pp. 72–73; Address before a Joint Session of the Congress on the State of the Union, January 29, 1991, *Weekly Compilation of Presidential Documents*, vol. 27, no. 5 (February 4, 1991), pp. 90–95; and Remarks to Community Members at Cherry Point Marine Corps Air Station in North Carolina, February 1, 1991, *Weekly Compilation of Presidential Documents*, vol. 27, no. 6 (February 11, 1991), pp. 109–110.

92. See Dinstein, *War, Aggression and Self-Defence*, supra note 57, pp. 61–69. Hugo Grotius was much occupied with just and unjust wars in his famous work on international law, first published in 1625, *De Jure Belli ac Pacis*, F.W. Kelsey, trans., *2 Classics of International Law* (Oxford: Oxford University Press, 1925).

93. For example, ibid., pp. 61–69; and Shaw, *International Law*, supra note 57, pp. 554–557.

94. Henkin, pp. 42–43 of this volume; Reisman, "Allocating Competences to Use Coercion in the Post–Cold War World," supra note 70, pp. 32–34; ———, "Coercion and Self-Determination: Construing Charter Article 2(4)," *American Journal of International Law*, vol. 78, no. 3 (1984), pp. 642–645; and ———,"Old Wine in New Bottles: The Reagan and Brezhnev Doctrines in Contemporary International Law and Practice," *Yale Journal of International Law*, vol. 13, no. 1 (1988), pp. 171–198.

95. "U.S.–Iraqi Talks Fail to Break Gulf Stalemate; Aziz Says War Would Bring Attack on Israel," *The Washington Post*, January 10, 1991, p. A1.

96. "UN Chief's Talks with Iraqis Bring No Sign of Change," *The New York Times*, January 14, 1991, p. A1.

97. "The Gulf Pollution Task Force," in *Hearing of the Senate Committee on Environment and Public Works*, Washington, D.C., Federal News Service transcript, July 11, 1991, and author's notes. (Testimony from this hearing is scheduled for publication by the Senate Committee on Environment and Public Works.)

98. Reports on the costs of and damage arising from the Gulf War appeared frequently in major newspapers and periodicals in the months following the cease-fire. A useful compilation of statistics and references to media reports is William M. Arkin, Damian Durrant, and Marianne Cherni, *On Impact: Modern Warfare and the Environment, A Case Study of the Gulf War* (Washington, D.C.: Greenpeace, May 1991).

99. One of the unfortunate omissions in the codified record of international law is a convention specifically regulating aerial bombing. However, one international agreement that never came into force but that reflects customary rules on warfare expressly covers the subject. See the 1923 Hague Rules of Aerial Warfare in Adam Roberts and Richard Guelff, eds., *Documents on the Laws of War*, 2nd ed. (New York: Oxford University

Press, 1989), pp. 121–135. Other agreements implicitly cover aerial warfare. The most relevant modern one is the 1977 Geneva Protocol I Additional to the Geneva Conventions of 12 August 1949, and Relating to the Protection of Victims of International Armed Conflicts (Part IV, Section I), printed in ibid., pp. 387 and 414–428. However, though the United States signed Geneva Protocol I under the Carter administration, the Reagan and Bush administrations have opposed its ratification in part because of objections to provisions that would bear upon aerial bombing.

100. On February 13, 1991, the U.S. air force executed a precise hit with two laser-guided bombs on a building in a residential neighborhood of Baghdad; Iraqi authorities later described the building as an air-raid shelter, while U.S. officials maintained it was an Iraqi military command center. Hundreds of civilians in the building reportedly were killed. See "Iraq Says U.S. Killed Hundreds of Civilians at Shelter, but Allies Call It Military Post," *The New York Times*, February 14, 1991, p. A1; and "Allies to Review Air Target Plans to Avoid Civilians," *The New York Times*, February 15, 1991, p. A1.

101. These international agreements are Geneva Convention I for the Amelioration of the Condition of the Wounded and Sick in Armed Forces in the Field; Geneva Convention II for the Amelioration of the Condition of Wounded, Sick and Shipwrecked Members of Armed Forces at Sea; Geneva Convention III Relative to the Treatment of Prisoners of War; and Geneva Convention IV Relative to the Protection of Civilian Persons in Time of War. See Roberts and Guelff, *Documents on the Laws of War,* supra note 99, pp. 169–337.

102. The 1977 Geneva Protocol I Additional to the Geneva Conventions of 12 August 1949, and Relating to the Protection of Victims of International Armed Conflicts; and Geneva Protocol II Additional to the Geneva Conventions of 12 August 1949, and Relating to the Protection of Victims of Non-International Armed Conflicts. Ibid., pp. 387–468.

103. These include the 1961 Vienna Convention on Diplomatic Relations (TIAS 7502) and the 1963 Vienna Convention on Consular Relations (TIAS 6820). In Resolution 667 (September 16, 1990), the UN Security Council found Iraq in violation of these conventions and demanded full compliance with them.

104. United Nations Document S/RES/670, September 25, 1990.

105. "Oil Spill, Growing Rapidly, Heads for Vital Saudi Sites; Air-War Goals Said to Shift," *The New York Times,* January 27, 1991, p. A1.

106. "Allied Forces Invade Kuwait as Bush Orders Ground War," *The Washington Post,* February 24, 1991, p. A1; and "Fighting the Great Balls of Fire," *The Washington Post,* April 1, 1991, p. D1.

107. United Nations General Assembly Resolution 44/39, December 4, 1989, paragraph 1.

108. United Nations General Assembly Resolution 3314, December 14, 1974. Reprinted in *International Legal Materials,* vol. 13 (1974), p. 710.

109. For a description of the International Law Commission's work on the Code through 1990, as well as its report to the General Assembly on the establishment of an international criminal court, see Stephen C.

McCaffrey, "The Forty-Second Session of the International Law Commission," *American Journal of International Law*, vol. 84, no. 4 (1990), pp. 930–936.

110. See Henkin, pp. 41–42 and 61 of this volume; Fernando R. Tesón, *Humanitarian Intervention: An Inquiry into Law and Morality* (Dobbs Ferry, N.Y.: Transnational Publishers, 1988); Richard B. Lillich, ed., *Humanitarian Intervention and the United Nations* (Charlottesville: University Press of Virginia, 1973); and Tom Farer, "An Inquiry into the Legitimacy of Humanitarian Intervention," in Damrosch and Scheffer, eds. *Law and Force in the New International Order*, supra note 70, pp. 185–201.

111. Examples typically suggested as evidence of an emerging rule of customary law on humanitarian intervention in response to mass violations of human rights are the Indian intervention in Bangladesh in 1971, the Vietnamese invasion (exclusive of the sustained occupation) of Cambodia in 1978, and the Tanzanian intervention in Uganda in 1979.

112. "Trail of Death in Iraq," *The Washington Post*, March 26, 1991, p. A1; "New Deaths, Destruction, Surround Ancient City," *The Washington Post*, March 28, 1991, p. A31.

113. United Nations Document S/RES/688, April 5, 1991. See "UN Tells Iraq to Halt Repression," *The Washington Post*, April 6, 1991, p. 1.

114. See The President's News Conference, April 16, 1991, *Weekly Compilation of Presidential Documents*, vol. 27, no. 16 (April 22, 1991), p. 444; White House Regular Briefing, Federal News Service transcript, April 17, 1991, p. 7; State Department Regular Briefing, Federal News Service transcript, April 18, 1991, p. 5; Jim Hoagland, "What Price Unity?" *The Washington Post*, May 14, 1991, p. A19; and Doris Meissner and David J. Scheffer, "No Manifesto for Armed Intervention," *The Washington Post*, May 28, 1991, p. A19.

115. "U.S. Insists It Won't Meddle in Iraq's Uprising," *The Los Angeles Times*, March 27, 1991, p. A1; State Department Regular Briefing, Federal News Service transcript, April 2, 1991, p. 4; "Bush, Aides Keep Quiet on Rebels," *The Washington Post*, April 3, 1991, p. 1; "Decision Not to Help Iraqi Rebels Puts U.S. in an Awkward Position," *The New York Times*, April 4, 1991, p. 1; "UN Nears Accord on Iraqi Killings: Bush Defends Hands-Off Policy," *The Washington Post*, April 5, 1991, p. 1; "Bush Orders Airlift of Aid to Refugees," *The Washington Post*, April 8, 1991, p. 1; "UN Buffer Zones in Iraq Suggested: Cheney Offers Idea to Safeguard Refugees," *The Washington Post*, April 8, 1991, p. 1. (On April 7, 1991, Defense Secretary Cheney stated on ABC's *This Week with David Brinkley* that the United States would "want to go back through the UN Security Council if in fact you're going to try to create some kind of mechanism or process that would provide an area there where [the Kurds would] be safe." Federal News Service transcript, April 7, 1991, p. 4. No further Security Council authorization, however, was obtained prior to the U.S. troop deployment in northern Iraq commencing in mid-April 1991.)

116. United Nations Document S/PV 2982, April 5, 1991.

117. See note 114.

118. White House Readout on Official Working Visit of UN Secretary General Pérez de Cuéllar, Briefer: John R. Bolton, Assistant Secretary of State for International Organization Affairs, The White House, Federal News Service transcript, May 9, 1991, WR-4-3E, p. 2.

119. Examples of this policy of denial and affirmation include the threat of military force to enforce the trade embargo against Iraq, followed by Resolution 665 (August 25, 1990); the threat of a counteroffensive against the Iraqi army to liberate Kuwait, followed by Resolution 678 (November 29, 1990); and the plan to arrange a cease-fire without Security Council involvement, followed by Resolution 686 (March 2, 1991) and Resolution 687 (April 3, 1991).

120. See *Congressional Record*, 102nd Cong., 1st Sess. (April 11, 1991), pp. S4325–S4327, S4333–S4334, S4385–S4386 [S. Res. 99].

121. "UN Takes Over from U.S. at the Kurdish Camp in Iraq," *The New York Times*, May 14, 1991, p. A10.

122. See note 73; "Cheney Sees Need to Act Militarily Against the Iraqis," *The New York Times*, December 4, 1990, p. A1; and Thomas Franck, "Declare War? Congress Can't," *The New York Times*, December 11, 1990, p. A27.

123. Compare Franck, "Declare War? Congress Can't" with Schachter, "Authorized Uses of Force by the United Nations and Regional Organizations," supra note 70, pp. 70–71.

124. "Votes Backing Use of Force Are Predicted in Congress," *The New York Times*, January 7, 1991, p. A11; "Bush Asks Congress to Back Force against Iraq," *The Washington Post*, January 9, 1991, p. A1; Letter to Congressional Leaders on the Persian Gulf Crisis, January 8, 1991, *Weekly Compilation of Presidential Documents*, vol. 27, no. 2 (January 14, 1991), p. 17. Government lawyers reportedly advised Bush on January 8, 1991, that he did not require congressional approval to launch Operation Desert Storm. See Bob Woodward, *The Commanders*, supra note 43, pp. 356–358.

125. The Senate and the House approved identical resolutions (S.J. Res. 2 and H.J. Res. 77, respectively) on January 12, 1991, and then the Senate approved the latter. See *Congressional Record*, 102nd Cong., 1st Sess. (January 12, 1991), pp. S369–S404, S413, and H443. The House resolution was assigned Public Law No. 102-1. See Statement on Signing the Resolution Authorizing the Use of Military Force against Iraq, January 14, 1991, *Weekly Compilation of Presidential Documents*, vol. 27, no. 3 (January 21, 1991), pp. 48–49. The Senate defeated S.J. Res. 1 by a vote of 52–47. The House defeated its counterpart, H. Con. Res. 33, by a vote of 250–183. *Congressional Record*, 102nd Cong., 1st Sess. (January 12, 1991), pp. S369–S404 and H405.

126. *Congressional Record*, 79th Cong., 1st Sess. (July 28, 1945), p. 8329.

127. Public Law No. 79-264, ch. 583, 59 Stat. 619 (1945) (22 USC Secs. 287-287e [1988]).

128. See Michael J. Glennon, "The Constitution and Chapter VII of the United Nations Charter," *American Journal of International Law*, vol. 85, no. 1 (1991), pp. 74–88; and War Powers and the UN Charter: Constitutional Roles of Congress and the President in Declaring and Waging War:

Hearings before the Senate Committee on the Judiciary, 102nd Cong., 1st Sess. Appendix (statement of David J. Scheffer)(scheduled for publication in 1991). A different interpretation appears in Thomas M. Franck and Faiza Patel, "UN Police Action in Lieu of War: 'The Old Order Changeth,' " *American Journal of International Law,* vol. 85, no. 1 (1991), pp. 63–73.

129. Remarks of Professor Peter Raven-Hansen at the 85th annual meeting of the American Society of International Law, Washington, D.C., April 17, 1991. (Proceedings of the meeting are scheduled for publication in early 1992.)

130. Section 3 of the UN Participation Act requires the U.S. delegate to the Security Council to vote in accordance with instructions from the president. During discussions on the UN Charter and the UN Participation Act in 1945, the Senate debated the delegation of this power to the president at considerable length and ultimately granted the president complete discretion.

131. See Statement on Signing the Resolution Authorizing the Use of Military Force against Iraq, January 14, 1991, *Weekly Compilation of Presidential Documents,* vol. 27, no. 3 (January 21, 1991), p. 48. Bush said, "As I made clear to congressional leaders at the outset, my request for congressional support did not, and my signing this resolution does not, constitute any change in the long-standing positions of the executive branch on either the President's constitutional authority to use the Armed Forces to defend vital U.S. interests or the constitutionality of the War Powers Resolution."

132. Address before a Joint Session of the Congress on the State of the Union, January 29, 1991, *Weekly Compilation of Presidential Documents,* vol. 27, no. 5 (February 4, 1991), p. 95.

133. Address before a Joint Session of the Congress on the Persian Gulf Crisis and the Federal Budget Deficit, September 11, 1990, *Weekly Compilation of Presidential Documents,* vol. 26, no. 37 (September 17, 1990), p. 1359.

134. Remarks at Maxwell Air Force Base War College in Montgomery, Alabama, April 13, 1991, *Weekly Compilation of Presidential Documents,* vol. 27, no. 16 (April 22, 1991), p. 431.

135. Speech by Pickering before the Veterans of Foreign Wars Meeting, Sheraton Washington Hotel, Washington, D.C., Federal News Service transcript, March 4, 1991, p. 3.

136. For a more thorough discussion of this issue, see Lori Fisler Damrosch, "Commentary on Collective Military Intervention to Enforce Human Rights," *Law and Force in the New International Order,* supra note 70, pp. 215–223.

137. Remarks by Senator Daniel Patrick Moynihan at the 85th annual meeting of the American Society of International Law, Washington, D.C., April 17, 1991.

AFTERWORD

John Temple Swing

Two and a half years after the original publication of *Right v. Might*, it is hard to overstate the significance of the dramatic events taking place in the world and the effect they have already had on the central issues dealt with in the chapters written then, at a time when most observers were just beginning to realize that the Cold War might indeed be rapidly drawing to an end.

One thing is clear: it would have been an omission of major proportions to publish a second edition of this work without exploring at least two events with special significance to international law and the use of force—the U.S. invasion of Panama on December 20, 1989, and the U.S.–led response to the Iraqi invasion of Kuwait on August 2, 1990. We are grateful to David Scheffer, who helped frame the issues in the first edition, for a new chapter analyzing those events from the perspective of the mainstream of international law.

Just one or two points of emphasis need be added here. The first concerns the centrality of the contribution of Mikhail S. Gorbachev. Only the events that unfolded in East Central Europe after publication could accurately measure the true significance of his December 7, 1988, speech to the United Nations on the rule of law, which both Scheffer and William Rogers noted in their earlier chapters. In country after country, revolutionary change, largely peaceful in nature, was allowed to proceed without the interposition of Soviet force that in the three previous decades would have been automatic. No other instance that comes readily to mind more aptly reflects the truth of the old adage that action (or, in this case, Soviet inaction) speaks even louder than (Mr. Gorbachev's) words.

Yet for our purposes, the ultimate significance of the Gorbachev-inspired "new thinking" came in a different guise. By committing his country to the rule of law in which "the use or threat of force no longer can be or must be an instrument of foreign policy," and "all of us . . . must . . . rule out any outward-oriented use of force,"[1] Gorbachev finally set the stage for the implementation of collective security as the framers of the United Nations Charter envisioned it. The days in which either superpower could be expected to block its opposite number by its veto in the Security Council had gone. The end of the automatic veto meant that provisions of the Charter that had lain moribund for forty-five years, particularly those found in Chapter VII, suddenly became available as a practical tool of international statecraft. We have already seen the first significant instance in the adoption without serious opposition of the multiple Security Council resolutions beginning in the immediate aftermath of the Iraqi invasion. More needs to be done, as Scheffer points out, almost certainly including the creation of an international rapid deployment force under the authority of the Security Council, but the central lesson remains. For the first time since the early days of the Cold War, the world has an opportunity to realize the goal of collective security as called for by the Charter.

What was the response of the United States to the challenge of Mr. Gorbachev's "new thinking"? It came in two parts, both of which Scheffer addresses—first "Panama"; then "Iraq." From the perspective of those who favor building international respect for the rule of law, the first represented a serious setback, the second a turnabout of almost 180 degrees. I would add to Scheffer's analysis of the illegalities of the Panama invasion only that, from a mainstream lawyer's perspective, what seemed its most pernicious aspect was not so much the invasion itself but the ex post facto attempts to provide a legal justification where, to state it baldly, in the opinion of most international lawyers, none existed. Perhaps worst of all, as Louis Henkin has pointed out elsewhere, was the distortion of the concept of self-defense by extending it to permit the use of force "whenever a state concludes that it is the victim of various forms of 'aggression' against

174

its 'vital interests' as it defines them, or that it has 'just cause.' "[2] Saddam Hussein relied on exactly that rationale to justify his invasion of Kuwait.

Iraq is another story. I remember vividly waking up on the morning of August 2 to the news of the Iraqi invasion of Kuwait. It provoked two immediate thoughts. The first was that the invasion was a crystal clear violation of Article 2(4) of the UN Charter, and of a sort that many analysts of international relations had believed would never occur again. Now international lawyers could stop arguing the fine points of the relative legalities among themselves. Perhaps more important, "realists" would no longer have cause to tell any international lawyer, as *The Wall Street Journal* did following the 1983 U.S. invasion of Grenada, to "keep his mouth shut"![3]

My second thought was that the invasion would have exactly the political consequences that the framers had feared in creating Article 2(4) in the first place: Iraq's resort to the massive use of force seriously upset the balance of power in the Middle East and thereby significantly threatened the "vital interests" of the world community, not just of the United States. It required an immediate response to avoid serious adverse consequences. Of these, perhaps the most dangerous was that Saddam Hussein would acquire a dominant position if the world acquiesced to his control of Kuwaiti oil reserves on top of Iraq's own. If he had also successfully overrun the Eastern Provinces of Saudi Arabia, as seemed possible and perhaps imminent in the days immediately following the invasion, the danger would have been even greater.

What happened is now history, and the main elements are well known. President Bush responded, but in spite of his unswerving rhetoric that reliance on the principle of "self-defense" required no further mandate than the invitation provided by Kuwait and Saudi Arabia, once the Security Council began to act, he launched Operation Desert Storm only after receiving authorization from the Council and the U.S. Congress. As Scheffer points out, without the adoption of Security Council Resolution 678, the outcome of what was a historic and commendable debate in the U.S. House of Representatives and Senate almost surely would have denied him the essential support of the American people for the launching of Desert Storm.

The turnaround in American thinking and policy is nowhere better captured than in a December 1990 statement by National Security Adviser Brent Scowcroft, who observed:

> This is a defining moment in world history. The cold war is over. We have the prospect of incipient cooperation among the major powers who have an inordinate responsibility for both the rule of law and peace and security in the world. If we can establish in this case the role of the United Nations, the role of the permanent Five, of the great powers, for the maintenance of an international order in the way that one should work to resolve disputes, then I think the next time it might be easier. A lot of people will be dissuaded from easy resort to force to solve their problems. And the next time, all it may take is a single U.N. resolution to solve the problem and not deployment of massive armed forces.[4]

"Realists" may argue that this, too, is no more than hollow rhetoric, and that "perceived national interest," not "idealistic" concepts of collective security, will always dictate policy. I believe they miss an important part of the picture. Collective security was never intended to operate in a vacuum. "Politics" and "political reality" were, are, and will continue to be an important factor. The two go, and indeed must go, together. I believe that it is in the enlightened self-interest of the United States to continue to develop and implement the collective security aspects of the Charter central to controlling the "use of force" under international law. To me the realpolitik mandate for this is clear. For one thing, we cannot afford to be the world's only policeman, just as we can no longer afford to be the principal funder of Third World development. This seems all the more certain when we do not even have the will to raise sufficient funds to satisfy crying domestic needs that have lain neglected far too long. For another, the United States is fundamentally a *status quo* power, and Article 2(4) is a *status quo*–preserving provision.

This is not to say that the road ahead does not contain plenty of pitfalls. One that deserves mention is the risk that Gorbachev and any reformers who follow him will essentially fail in their attempts to reform the economy and politics of the Soviet Union. Although it seems unlikely, one cannot rule out the emergence of a strongly nationalistic, chauvinistic regime willing to reject "new thinking" and return to reliance on the primacy of military power as the source of its authority. Such a regime almost by definition would be a danger to world stability. At the very least, it could well return us to the days of superpower confrontation and automatic vetoes in the Security Council that were the hallmark of the Cold War.

Furthermore, numerous questions remain unanswered. One of the most interesting and timely is to what extent the international community will sanction interference in the internal affairs of a sovereign state for humanitarian purposes, including the prevention of genocide (the risk of which continues to exist in Kurdistan) or famine (in Ethiopia and the Sudan). As Scheffer points out, we began to see an interesting evolution away from the time-honored rule against such interference in the case of Iraq and its treatment of the Kurds. A related but different question that is bound to vex the world community is how the competition between the principles of "nonintervention," enshrined in Article 2(7) of the Charter, and "self-determination" will play itself out. These two principles clashed in Yugoslavia in 1991 and may soon again in the Soviet Union. Yet, as important as they are, such questions are subsidiary to the main issues involving control of the aggressive use of force this volume addresses.

Still to be resolved, however, is the ancient question of peaceful change: If drastic change in the world is no longer to be allowed to flow from the barrel of a gun, how can it take place in the international system? Certainly part of the answer lies in the strengthening of international institutions (the General Agreement on Tariffs and Trade, World Bank, International Court of Justice, and so on) or the creation of new ones where the essential mechanisms for peaceful evolution and growth do not exist. Without such institutions and without an international consensus on the need to stop the aggressive use of force, as the Charter contemplates, the alternative is stark. It is to go back to the not so very good old days of "might makes right," the essence of which Wordsworth captured so well in his poem "Rob Roy's Grave":

> The good old rule
> . . . the simple plan,
> That they should take, who have the power,
> And they should keep who can.[5]

August 1991

NOTES

1. Statement by Mikhail S. Gorbachev at Plenary Meeting of the United Nations General Assembly, December 7, 1988, provided by the Embassy of the USSR, Washington, D.C. A full text of the statement also is reprinted in *Foreign Broadcast Information Service—Soviet Union*, vol. 88, no. 236 (December 8, 1988), pp. 11–19.
2. Louis Henkin, "The Invasion of Panama under International Law: A Gross Violation," *Columbia Journal of Transnational Law*, vol. 29 (1991).
3. "Lawyers Invade Grenada," *The Wall Street Journal*, November 1, 1983, p. 30.
4. Interview with Senior Editor Kenneth T. Walsh, *U.S. News & World Report*, December 24, 1990, p. 27.
5. Quoted in Daniel Patrick Moynihan, *On the Law of Nations* (Boston: Harvard University Press, 1990), p. 4.

APPENDIX

*Council on Foreign Relations Study Group on
International Law and the Use of Force:
Implications for U.S. Foreign Policy*

February 1985–July 1988

William D. Rogers (Chairman), *Partner, Arnold & Porter*
John Temple Swing (Director), *Executive Vice President,
Council on Foreign Relations*
David J. Scheffer (Rapporteur), *Associate, Coudert Brothers*

Zoe Baird, *O'Melveny & Myers*
Barry M. Blechman, *Georgetown University*
Abram J. Chayes, *Harvard University*
William E. Colby, *Colby Bailey Werner & Associates*
Lloyd N. Cutler, *Wilmer Cutler & Pickering*
Lori F. Damrosch, *Columbia University*
Thomas M. Franck, *New York University*
Richard N. Gardner, *Columbia University*
Allan Gerson, *U.S. Department of State*
Gidon A.G. Gottlieb, *University of Chicago*
Ernest A. Gross, *Curtis Mallet-Prevost Colt & Mosle*
John L. Hargrove, *American Society of International Law*
Louis Henkin, *Columbia University*
Keith Highet, *Curtis Mallet-Prevost Colt & Mosle*
Stanley Hoffmann, *Harvard University*
Milton Katz, *Harvard University*
Nicholas deB. Katzenbach, *IBM Corporation*
Robert M. Kimmit, *National Security Council*
Jeane J. Kirkpatrick, *American Enterprise Institute*
Paul H. Kreisberg, *Council on Foreign Relations*

Karl E. Meyer, *The New York Times*
Adam Meyerson, *Policy Review*
John Norton Moore, *University of Virginia*
Daniel P. Moynihan, *U.S. Senator from New York*
Joseph S. Nye, Jr., *Harvard University*
Robert J. Pranger, *American Enterprise Institute*
Susan Kaufman Purcell, *Council on Foreign Relations*
W.M. Reisman, *Yale University*
Eugene V. Rostow, *National Defense University*
Oscar Schachter, *Columbia University*
Arthur Schlesinger, Jr., *City University of New York*
Enid C.B. Schoettle, *Ford Foundation*
Stephen M. Schwebel, *International Court of Justice*
Abraham D. Sofaer, *U.S. Department of State*
Louis B. Sohn, *University of Georgia*
John R. Stevenson, *Sullivan & Cromwell*
Robert B. von Mehren, *Debevoise & Plimpton*

MEETINGS

February 28, 1985
U.S. and USSR: Demonstrative Uses of Military Power
Discussion Leaders:
Barry Blechman, *President, Defense Forecasts, Inc.*
Louis Henkin, *Professor of Law, Columbia University*

March 26, 1985
Managing U.S.–Soviet Rivalry: Problems of Crisis Prevention
Discussion Leader:
Alexander L. George, *Professor of International Relations, Stanford University*

April 23, 1985
The Role Courts can Play in Issues Regarding Use of Force
Discussion Leaders:
Ernest A. Gross, *Of Counsel, Curtis Mallet-Prevost Colt & Mosle*
Stephen W. Schwebel, *Judge, International Court of Justice*

June 13, 1985
International Law and the Use of Force: The Interests of the
United States
Discussion Leaders:
Louis Henkin, *Professor of Law, Columbia University*
Oscar Schachter, *Professor of Law, Columbia University*

November 2, 1987
An Analysis of the World Court Decision in the Nicaragua Case
—Part I
Discussion Leader:
Oscar Schachter, *Professor of Law, Columbia University*

December 14, 1987
An Analysis of the World Court Decision in the Nicaragua Case
—Part II
Discussion Leader:
Keith Highet, *Partner, Curtis Mallet-Prevost Colt & Mosle*

March 16, 1988
The Use of Force in Connection with U.S. Policy in Central
America
Discussion Leaders:
Tom Farer, *Professor of Law, University of New Mexico*
Nancy Kassebaum, *U.S. Senator from Kansas*

July 25, 1988
Authors' Review

*Note: Study group members' affiliations are listed as they were when
   participant first joined the group.*

SUGGESTED READINGS

"Agora: The Downing of Iran Air Flight 655." *American Journal of International Law* 83, no. 2 (1989): pp. 318–341.

"Agora: The Gulf Crisis in International and Foreign Relations Law." *American Journal of International Law* 85, no. 1 (1991): pp. 63–109.

"Agora: U.S. Forces in Panama: Defenders, Aggressors or Human Rights Activists?" *American Journal of International Law* 84, no. 2 (1990): pp. 494–524.

The American Law Institute. "Unilateral Remedies." In *Restatement (Third) of the Foreign Relations Law of the United States* 2, sec. 905, pp. 380–392. St. Paul: American Law Institute Publishers, 1987.

Aron, Raymond. *Peace and War.* New York: Doubleday, 1966.

Bilder, Richard B., et al. "The United Nations Charter and the Use of Force: Is Article 2(4) Still Workable?" In *Proceedings of the Seventy-Eighth Annual Meeting of The American Society of International Law,* pp. 68–107. Washington, D.C.: The American Society of International Law, 1986.

Bork, Robert H. "The Limits of 'International Law.'" *The National Interest,* no. 18 (Winter 1989/90): pp. 3–10.

Bowett, Derek. "Reprisals Involving Recourse to Armed Force." *American Journal of International Law* 66, no. 1 (1972): pp. 1–36.

———. *Self-Defense in International Law.* Manchester: Manchester University Press, 1958.

Boyle, Francis A., et al. "Letter: International Lawlessness in Grenada." *American Journal of International Law* 78, no. 1 (1984): pp. 172–175.

Brownlie, Ian. *International Law and the Use of Force by States.* New York: Oxford University Press, 1963.

Butler, W. E., ed. "The Non-Use of Force in International Law." *Coexistence* 26, no. 1 (March 1989): whole issue.

Chayes, Abram. *The Cuban Missile Crisis.* New York: Oxford University Press, 1974.

———. "Nicaragua, The United States, and the World Court." *Columbia Law Review* 85, no. 7 (1985): pp. 1445–1482.

Cohen, Eliot A. "The Future of Force and American Strategy." *The National Interest,* no. 21 (Fall 1990): pp. 3–15.

Cutler, Lloyd N. "The Right to Intervene." *Foreign Affairs* 64, no. 1 (1985): pp. 96–122.

Damrosch, Lori Fisler. "Politics Across Borders: Nonintervention and Nonforcible Influence over Domestic Affairs." *American Journal of International Law* 83, no. 1 (1989): pp. 1–50.

———, ed. *The International Court of Justice at a Crossroads.* Dobbs Ferry: Transnational Publishers, 1987.

Damrosch, Lori Fisler and David J. Scheffer, eds. *Law and Force in the New International Order.* Boulder: Westview Press, 1991.

Dinstein, Yoram. *War, Aggression and Self-Defence.* Cambridge: Grotius Publications Limited, 1988.

Falk, Richard A., ed., *The Vietnam War and International Law* 1–4. Princeton: Princeton University Press, 1968, 1969, 1972, 1976.

Farer, Tom J. "International Law: The Critics are Wrong." *Foreign Policy,* no. 71 (Summer 1988): pp. 22–45.

Fisher, Roger. *Improving Compliance with International Law.* Charlottesville: University Press of Virginia, 1981.

Franck, Thomas M. "Dulce et Decorum Est: The Strategic Role of Legal Principles in the Falklands War." *American Journal of International Law* 77, no. 1 (1983): pp. 109–124.

―――. "Who Killed Article 2(4)? Or: Changing Norms Governing the Use of Force by States." *American Journal of International Law* 64, no. 3 (1970): pp. 809–907.

Friedmann, Wolfgang. "Intervention and International Law." *International Spectator* 25, no. 1 (1971): pp. 40–66.

Gardner, Richard N. "The Case for Practical Internationalism." *Foreign Affairs* 66, no. 4 (1988): pp. 827–845.

―――. "Sovereignty and Intervention: A Challenge of Law-Making for the Industrialized Democracies." *Trialogue,* no. 35 (Winter 1984): pp. 3–12.

―――, et al. "Armed Force, Peaceful Settlements, and the United Nations Charter: Are There Alternatives to 'A New International Anarchy?'" In *Proceedings of the Seventy-Seventh Annual Meeting of The American Society of International Law,* pp. 31–51. Washington, D.C.: The American Society of International Law, 1985.

George, Alexander L., ed. *Managing U.S.–Soviet Rivalry.* Boulder: Westview Press, 1983.

George, Alexander L.; Philip J. Farley; and Alexander Dallin, eds. *U.S.–Soviet Security Cooperation.* New York: Oxford University Press, 1988.

Glennon, Michael J. "The Gulf War and the Constitution." *Foreign Affairs* 70, no. 2 (Spring 1991): pp. 84–101.

Graham, Gordon. "The justice of intervention." *Review of International Studies* 13 (April 1987): pp. 133–146.

Halperin, Morton H. "Lawful Wars." *Foreign Policy,* no. 72 (Fall 1988): pp. 173–195.

Henkin, Louis. "Foreign Affairs and the Constitution." *Foreign Affairs* 66, no. 2 (1987/88): pp. 284–310.

———. *How Nations Behave,* 2d ed. New York: Columbia University Press, 1979.

———. "The Reports of the Death of Article 2(4) are Greatly Exaggerated." *American Journal of International Law* 65, no. 3 (1971): pp. 544–548.

———. "The Invasion of Panama under International Law: A Gross Violation. *Columbia Journal of Transnational Law,* vol. 29 (1991).

Highet, Keith. "Evidence, the Court, and the Nicaragua Case." *American Journal of International Law* 81, no. 1 (1987): pp. 1–56.

Hoffmann, Stanley. *Duties beyond Borders: On the Limits and Possibilities of Ethical International Politics.* Syracuse: Syracuse University Press, 1981.

———. "International Law and the Control of Force." In Karl Deutsch and Stanley Hoffmann, eds., *The Relevance of International Law,* pp. 34–66. New York: Doubleday, Anchor Books, 1971.

———. *Janus and Minerva.* Boulder: Westview Press, 1986.

Hoyt, Edwin C. *Law & Force in American Foreign Policy.* Lanham, New York: University Press of America, 1985.

Johnson, Robert H. "Misguided Morality: Ethics and the Reagan Doctrine." *Political Science Quarterly* 103, no. 3 (1988): pp. 509–529.

———. *Rollback Revisited: A Reagan Doctrine for Insurgent Wars?* Washington, D.C.: Overseas Development Council, January 1986.

Joyner, Christopher O. "Reflections on the Lawfulness of Invasion." *American Journal of International Law* 78, no. 1 (1984): pp. 131–144.

Keohane, Robert. "Reciprocity in International Relations," *International Organization* 40, no. 1 (1986): pp. 1–27.

Kirkpatrick, Jeane J. *Implementing the Reagan Doctrine.* National Security Record No. 82. Washington, D.C.: The Heritage Foundation, August 1985.

———. "Law and Reciprocity." In *Proceedings of the Seventy-Eighth Annual Meeting of The American Society of International Law,* pp. 59–68. Washington, D.C.: The American Society of International Law, 1986.

———. *The Reagan Doctrine and U.S. Foreign Policy.* Washington, D.C.: The Heritage Foundation, 1985.

Krauthammer, Charles. "The Curse of Legalism." *The New Republic,* November 6, 1989, pp. 44–50.

———. "Morality and the Reagan Doctrine: The rights and wrongs of guerilla war." *The New Republic,* September 8, 1986, pp. 17–24.

————. "The Poverty of Realism: The newest challenge to the Reagan Doctrine." *The New Republic,* February 17, 1986, pp. 14–22.

Leigh, Monroe, et al. "Legal and Political Issues in the Central American Conflict." In *Proceedings of the Seventy-Ninth Annual Meeting of The American Society of International Law,* pp. 40–57. Washington, D.C.: The American Society of International Law, 1987.

Levitin, Michael J. "The Law of Force and the Force of Law: Grenada, the Falklands, and Humanitarian Intervention." *Harvard International Law Journal* 27, no. 2 (1986): pp. 621–657.

Liska, George. "The Reagan Doctrine: Monroe and Dulles Reincarnate?" *SAIS Review* 6, no. 2 (1986): pp. 83–98.

Lowenfeld, Andreas F. " U.S. Law Enforcement Abroad: The Constitution and International Law." *American Journal of International Law* 83, no. 4 (1989): pp. 880–893.

————. "U.S. Law Enforcement Abroad: The Constitution and International Law Continued." *American Journal of International Law* 84, no. 2 (1990): pp. 444–493.

Maechling, Charles Jr. "Washington's Illegal Invasion." *Foreign Policy,* no. 79 (Summer 1990): pp. 113–131.

Maier, Harold G., ed. "Appraisals of the ICJ's Decision: Nicaragua v. United States (Merits)." *American Journal of International Law* 81, no. 1 (1987): pp. 77–183.

Moore, John Norton. "Grenada and the International Double Standard." *American Journal of International Law* 78, no. 1 (1984): pp. 145–168.

————. "The Secret War in Central America and the Future of World Order." *American Journal of International Law* 80, no. 1 (1986): pp. 43–127.

————, ed. *Law and Civil War in the Modern World.* Baltimore: The Johns Hopkins University Press, 1974.

Morgenthau, Hans J. *Politics Among Nations,* 6th ed., rev. Kenneth W. Thompson. New York: Alfred A. Knopf, 1985.

Moynihan, Daniel P. *Loyalties.* New York: Harcourt Brace Jovanovich, 1984.

————. *On the Law of Nations.* Cambridge: Harvard University Press, 1990.

Mullerson, R. A. "Sources of International Law: New Tendencies in Soviet Thinking." *American Journal of International Law* 83, no. 3 (1989): pp. 494–512.

Muravchik, Joshua. "Maximum Feasible Containment: The Reagan Doctrine after Iranamok." *The New Republic,* June 1, 1987, pp. 23–25.

Nye, Joseph S., Jr. *Nuclear Ethics.* New York: Free Press, 1986.

Paust, Jordan J. "Entebbe and Self-Help." *The Fletcher Forum* 2, no. 1 (1978): pp. 86–92.

Perkins, John A. *The Prudent Peace: Law as Foreign Policy.* Chicago: The University of Chicago Press, 1981.

————. "The Right of Counterrevolution." *Georgia Journal of International & Comparative Law* 17, no. 2 (1986): pp. 171–227.

Reisman, W. Michael. "Coercion and Self-Determination: Construing Charter Article 2(4)." *American Journal of International Law* 78, no. 3 (1984): pp. 642–645.

———. "International Law after the Cold War." *American Journal of International Law* 84, no. 4 (1990): pp. 859–865.

———. "Old Wine in New Bottles: The Reagan and Brezhnev Doctrines in Contemporary International Law and Practice." *Yale Journal of International Law* 13, no. 1 (1988): pp. 171–198.

Rosenfeld, Stephen S. "The Guns of July." *Foreign Affairs* 64, no. 4 (1986): pp. 698–714.

Rostow, Nicholas. "Law and the Use of Force by States: The Brezhnev Doctrine." *The Yale Journal of World Public Order* 7, no. 2 (1981): pp. 209–243.

Rowles, James P. " 'Secret Wars,' Self-Defense and the Charter— A Reply to Professor Moore." *American Journal of International Law* 80, no. 3 (1986): pp. 568–583.

Rubin, Seymour J., et al. "World Court Jurisdiction and U.S. Foreign Policy in Latin America." In *Proceedings of the Seventy-Eighth Annual Meeting of The American Society of International Law*, pp. 321–337. Washington, D.C.: The American Society of International Law, 1986.

Russett, Bruce and James S. Sutterlin. "The U.N. in the New World Order." *Foreign Affairs* 70, no. 2 (Spring 1991): pp. 69–83.

Sadurska, Romana. "Threats of Force." *American Journal of International Law* 82, no. 2 (1988): pp. 239–268.

Schachter, Oscar. *International Law in Theory and Practice*, pp. 133–187. Boston: Martinus Nijhoff, 1985.

———. "Is There a Right to Overthrow an Illegitimate Regime?" *Le Droit international au service de la paix, de la justice et du développement*, pp. 424–430. Paris: Melanges Michel Virally, 1991.

———. "The Legality of Pro-Democratic Invasion." *American Journal of International Law* 78, no. 3 (1984): pp. 645–650.

———. "The Right of States to Use Armed Force." *Michigan Law Review* 82, nos. 5–6 (April–May 1984): pp. 1620–1646.

———. "Self-Defense and the Rule of Law." *American Journal of International Law* 83, no. 2 (1989): pp. 259–277.

Scheffer, David J. "Nouveau Law and Foreign Policy." *Foreign Policy*, no. 76 (Fall 1989): pp. 44–65.

———. "The United Nations in the Gulf Crisis and Options for U.S. Foreign Policy." Occasional Paper No. 1. New York: United Nations Association of the U.S.A., October 1990.

Singh, J.N. *Use of Force Under International Law.* New Delhi: Harnam Publications, 1984.

Sofaer, Abraham D. "International Law and the Use of Force." *The National Interest,* no. 13 (Fall 1988): pp. 53–64.

———. "The Legality of the United States' Action in Panama." *Columbia Journal of Transnational Law,* vol. 29 (1991).

———. "Terrorism and the Law." *Foreign Affairs* 64, no. 5 (1986): pp. 901–922.

Solarz, Stephen J. "When to Intervene." *Foreign Policy,* no. 63 (Summer 1986): pp. 20–39.

Tesón, Fernando R. *Humanitarian Intervention: An Inquiry Into Law and Morality.* Dobbs Ferry: Transnational Publishers, 1988.

Tucker, Robert W., ed. *Intervention and the Reagan Doctrine.* New York: Council on Religion and International Affairs, 1985.

Tunkin, Grigori. *Law and Force in the International System.* Moscow: Progress Publishers, 1985.

Turner, Robert F. "International Law, the Reagan Doctrine, and World Peace: Going Back to the Future." *The Washington Quarterly* 11, no. 4 (1988): pp. 119–136.

United Nations. *The Blue Helmets: A Review of United Nations Peacekeeping.* Second Edition. New York: 1990.

U.S. Congress. *Report of the Congressional Committee Investigating the Iran-Contra Affair.* 100th Cong. 1st Sess., November 1987. H. Rept. 100–433, S. Rept. 100–216.

U.S. Department of State. *Revolution Beyond Our Borders: Sandinista Intervention in Central America.* Special Report 132. 1985.

Vagts, Detlev F. "International Law under Time Pressure: Grading the Grenada Take-Home Examination." *American Journal of International Law* 78, no. 1 (1984): pp. 169–172.

Waldock, C.H.M. "The Regulation of the Use of Force by Individual States in International Law." *Recueil des cours* 81, no. II (1952): pp. 451–517.

Wallace, Don, Jr. "International Law and the Use of Force: Reflections on the Need for Reform." *The International Lawyer* 19, no. 1 (1985): pp. 259–275.

Walzer, Michael. *Just and Unjust Wars.* New York: Basic Books, 1977.

INDEX

ABOUT THE AUTHORS

Allan Gerson is currently of counsel at Hughes Hubbard & Reed. He was a resident scholar at the American Enterprise Institute (1985–1989); deputy assistant attorney general (1985–1986); and counsel to the U.S. mission of the United Nations (1981–1985).

Louis Henkin is currently university professor emeritus and special service professor at Columbia University. He is also president of the United States Institute of Human Rights and a member of the Executive Committee of the Lawyers Committee for Human Rights. He has served as an advisor on international law to the U.S. Department of State and to the U.S. delegation on the law of the sea, and as co-editor-in-chief of *The American Journal of International Law.*

Stanley Hoffmann is Douglas Dillon Professor of the Civilization of France at Harvard University, where he has taught since 1955. He has been the chairman of the Center for European Studies since its creation in 1969. Among the many books of which he is the author or co-author are *Duties beyond Borders, Janus and Minerva,* and *The Mitterand Experiment.*

Jeane J. Kirkpatrick is the Leavey Professor of Government at Georgetown University and a senior fellow at the American Enterprise Institute. From 1981 to 1985, she served as the U.S. permanent representative to the United Nations.

William D. Rogers is senior partner at Arnold & Porter. He was previously undersecretary of state for economic affairs from 1976 to 1977; assistant secretary of state for inter-American affairs from 1974 to 1976; and president of The American Society for International Law from 1972 to 1974.

David J. Scheffer is a senior associate of the Carnegie Endowment for International Peace, where he specializes in international and national security law. He is a former staff consultant of the House Committee on Foreign Affairs, and from 1979 to 1986 was an associate attorney in the New York and Singapore offices of Coudert Brothers, an international law firm.